TEXAS

◆

STYLE

TEXAS · STYLE

COOKING, GARDENING, AND ENTERTAINING IN THE LONE STAR STATE

CONNIE SHERLEY

CRESCENT BOOKS
NEW YORK / AVENEL, NEW JERSEY

A FRIEDMAN GROUP BOOK

This 1992 edition published by Crescent Books, distributed by Outlet Book Company, Inc., a Random House Company, 40 Engelhard Avenue, Avenel, New Jersey 07001.

ISBN 0-517-05178-8

TEXAS STYLE
Cooking, Gardening, and Entertaining in the Lone Star State
was prepared and produced by
Michael Friedman Publishing Group, Inc.
15 West 26th Street
New York, New York 10010

Art Director: Jeff Batzli
Designer: Maria Avitabile
Photography Editor: Ede Rothaus

Typeset by Bookworks Plus
Color separations by Excel Graphic Arts Ltd.
Printed and bound in Hong Kong by Leefung-Asco Printers Ltd.

8 7 6 5 4 3 2 1

Additional Photographs:
p p. 14 © Jack Zehrt/F.P.G. International
p p. 44 © Gary Buss/F.P.G. International
p p. 112 © Wyman P. Meinzer

Acknowledgments

I owe special thanks to Rosemary Williams, senior editor of *Texas Highways,* for suggesting that I write this book and generously providing me with a wealth of Texana materials; to Ruthmary Jordan and Derro Evans for updates on Jefferson; to Susan Teeple Auler of Fall Creek Vineyards, Lucy Fox, and Peggy Buzan for recipe contributions; to Marilyn and John R. Thomas of Wildseed for sharing information about wildflowers and native plants; and to my research assistant, Ruth Hester, for her priceless knowledge, patience, persistence, and sense of humor.

Dedication

This book is dedicated to my indomitable research assistant, Ruth Hester, whose knowledge of Texana challenges me; to Frank Lively and the *Texas Highways* staff, who brought me back to my travel writing roots; and to G.Q., who makes everything possible.

CONTENTS

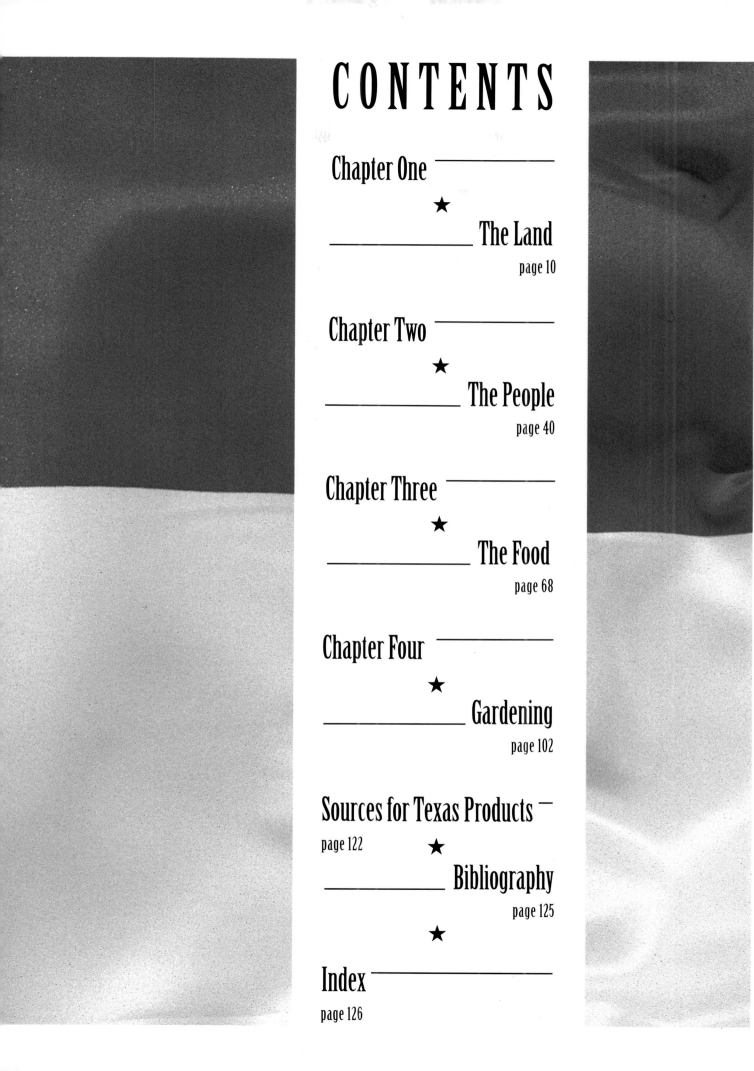

Chapter One

★

The Land
page 10

Chapter Two

★

The People
page 40

Chapter Three

★

The Food
page 68

Chapter Four

★

Gardening
page 102

Sources for Texas Products
page 122   ★

Bibliography
page 125

★

Index
page 126

THE LAND

If you think Texas is big today, consider this: In 1850, the state's boundaries stretched west across much of present-day New Mexico and north through portions of Oklahoma, Colorado, Kansas, and Wyoming. The sparsely populated state had so much territory and so little money, settlers were paying less than one dollar an acre for prime land and actually being given acreage to move into wilderness areas.

Although the state had no documents to back its claim that the Rio Grande—from its headwaters to the Gulf of Mexico—was Texas' legal, far-flung boundary, the debt-ridden government ran the bluff for four years, and finally won the gamble when the United States paid ten million dollars to settle the issue so the nation's westward expansion could continue.

Colorado's Rocky Mountain ski country would be part of Texas today if it hadn't been for that real estate coup—called the Compromise of 1850—which cut the state to its present size and distinctive shape and reduced the length of the Rio Grande boundary to 1,270 miles.

There's still plenty of land between Texline in the north and Brownsville, 890 miles to the south, and the Sabine River in the east and the Rio Grande at El Paso, 773 miles west. Texans delight in telling tales about ranches with several zip codes and how you could tuck Great Britain into Texas and still have two-thirds of the state left over.

All that territory encompasses a distinctive variety of terrain and climates. In January when Panhandle residents are shoveling snow, their Rio Grande Valley counterparts are harvesting the citrus crop. An annual average rainfall of fifty-nine inches keeps the boggy Big Thicket in East Texas lush, while West Texas stays dry with only eight inches of rain each year. Despite its arid image, Texas has more inland lakes than any of the contiguous states, including Minnesota.

The six flags that decorate everything from the Texas Capitol to an amusement park represent the nations that have laid claim to the land: Spain (1519 to 1685 and 1690 to 1821), France (1685 to 1690), Mexico (1821 to 1836), the Republic (1836 to 1845), the United States (1845 to 1861 and 1865 to the present), and the Confederacy (1861 to 1865). Each era helped mold the state as Texans know it today, although there are those who claim Texas is still being invented.

When the upstart republic agreed to annexation in 1845, Texas retained ownership and control of public lands that covered almost 179 million acres. Eventually The University of Texas and its branches received an allotment of 2.3 million acres as a permanent fund. Yes, capitalization of "The" was included in the constitutional amendment. Most of the school's paltry profits came from grazing rights until 1923, when the Santa Rita well in far West Texas sparked a chain of oil and gas development on university land. The rig that put the U.T. system on the road to riches is enshrined in a corner of the Austin campus.

The statehood pact also gave Texas the right to divide its lands into as many as five states, but no one expects that ever to happen. Who would get the Alamo?

Trans Pecos

The Trans Pecos region, that area of far West Texas where the Chihuahuan Desert begins and the Rio Grande becomes the U.S.-Mexico border, fits the Texas stereotype of endless, barren land—with remarkable exceptions.

Guadalupe Mountains National Park boasts the highest point in Texas, Guadalupe Peak, an 8,751-foot outcropping topped with dark green ponderosa pines. The Trans Pecos has ninety-one mountains that are a mile or more high, as well as the irrigated fields of the fertile Pecos River Valley that produce succulent fruits.

RIGHT: *In the spring thousands of cacti blossoms, from the low-lying, hot pink pitaya to the towering, creamy white dagger plant, produce a riot of color throughout Big Bend National Park.* CENTER: *The Guadalupe Mountains rise above the Chihuahuan Desert along the Texas–New Mexico border. For years El Capitan (8,078 feet) was thought to be the state's highest mountain, but that title goes to nearby Guadalupe Peak (8,751 feet).*

© David Langford

Big Bend National Park, nestled in the curve where rampaging waters of the now-tame Rio Grande carved spectacular canyons when the river twisted to the north, is one of America's last great wilderness preserves. The park also is a Texas-size cactus garden, with more than 850 varieties within its 775,243 acres. If you picture deserts only in earth tones, Big Bend will color those mental images. When spring rains drift through the usually arid areas, purple cholla blossoms contrast with snowball cacti. The pitaya becomes a bouquet of hot pink flowers with deep gold centers, and creamy white blossoms burst from dagger plant stalks.

Encircled by 100 miles of desert, El Paso, the region's urban hub, developed because commerce and traffic could flow through a natural cut in the Rocky Mountain foothills that the Spanish called "El Paso del Norte," meaning the Great Pass of the North, and precious fresh water always could be found in rock basins, which caught and stored the meager amount of annual rainfall.

Ysleta Mission, established in 1681, still serves the Tigua Indians living nearby at Ysleta del Sur Pueblo, Texas' oldest settlement, now very much a part of colorful El Paso and its Latin-beat lifestyle.

The remote city is even in a different time zone, so the rest of Texas is always an hour ahead. El Paso and its sister city, Juárez, across the Rio Grande, form a bilingual metropolitan center of more than 1.5 million people.

LEFT: *Palm trees and tropical plantings border "resacas" the rampaging Rio Grande carved through the lush valley separating Texas from Mexico.* **FOLLOWING PAGE:** *The Indians called the Big Bend's gigantic outcroppings* chisos, *for "ghosts," because the light plays such lovely tricks on the mountains, turning the rugged rocks blue and gray in early morning; golden in full sunlight; and hues of bronze, blue, and pink at sunset.*

Rio Grande Valley

For centuries the mighty Rio Grande pushed tons of rich silt hundreds of miles and cast the fertile soil aside before rendezvousing with the Gulf of Mexico at the southern tip of Texas. The fruitful floods also left lagoons, called *resacas*, winding through the area like watery ribbons.

Dams eventually tamed the Rio Grande into a rather listless stream, but the land's legacy continues. Palm trees, vivid bougainvillea, and hibiscus border the resacas; citrus orchards cover thousands of acres. Another famous product, the 1015 onion, named for the October planting date, is sweet enough to eat like an apple.

Winter usually is marked more by the calendar than the temperature in the Rio Grande Valley, although the Texas weather can play mighty cruel tricks. Gulf breezes constantly rattle the palm fronds and cool the long, hot summers.

could be exchanged for arms and munitions. The last land battle of the Civil War was fought twelve miles east of the port at Palmito Ranch, an area so remote the force commanded by Colonel John S. Ford routed and captured 113 Union troops on May 13, 1865, only to learn from their prisoners that General Robert E. Lee had surrendered the preceding April 9.

On the other side of the river the Rio Grande becomes Rio Bravo in Matamoros, Brownsville's sister city. "Howdy" and "Buenos días," are interchangeable greetings in the bilingual culture.

© Steve Bentsen

OPPOSITE PAGE: *Boats of all sizes and descriptions moor at the marinas alongside Corpus Christi's business district. At noon, brown baggers share their lunches with the city's famed "laughing gulls," graceful, gliding birds that always seem to be reacting to a ribald joke.* **INSET:** *Hobie cats provide recreation at Padre Island.* **LEFT:** *The Queen Isabella Causeway curls across Laguna Madre from Port Isabel on the mainland to the southern tip of Padre Island.*

The valley is the gateway to the southern tip of Padre Island—the long, skinny barrier stretching 113 miles from Corpus Christi to Port Isabel. Laguna Madre—the Mother Lake—separates the mainland from Padre Island, which is split thirty-four miles from its southern tip by the Mansfield Cut, a manmade channel to the Gulf of Mexico. The Queen Isabella Causeway, the state's longest bridge, provides access to South Padre. From the first week in March through Easter thousands of students on spring break invade the beach resort.

Brownsville, the valley's largest city, and Miami, Florida, are on the same latitude. A seventeen-mile ship channel connecting the port with the ocean makes Brownsville the terminus of the Gulf Intracoastal Waterway system and home of one of the world's largest shrimp fleets. During the Civil War, Brownsville became a crucial Confederate outlet for shipping Southern cotton through Mexico to Europe, where it

South Texas Brush Country

Cattle ranching in North America began on the grassy plains north of the Rio Grande Valley, called the "Brush Country" because of the mesquite, oak, and cacti dotting the land. Many of the ranchers trace ownership of their spreads to Spanish land grants acquired by Mexican ancestors in the eighteenth century.

The Rincon de Santa Gertrudis, a 15,500-acre Spanish land grant, became the nucleus of the world-famous King Ranch in 1852, when Richard King bought the land from the original owners for three hundred dollars. Today the fabled spread's four divisions cover 825,000 acres, which require 2,000 miles of fencing and 500 miles of paved roads, plus countless untopped trails.

© L. Rue, Jr./FPG International

TOP: *Valley quail are among the indigenous birds sought by hunters who invade the Brush Country every autumn.* **BOTTOM:** *Twisted mesquites form a fence line through the South Texas Brush Country.* **OPPOSITE PAGE:** *Branding time on a South Texas ranch.*

A ranch's brand is its coat of arms, designed to be easily recognized and difficult for rustlers and other rascals to alter. The King Ranch's Running W hallmark is known throughout the world.

As they moved across the coastal plains, the conquistadors left domestic animals at river crossings to ensure a supply of fresh meat when they returned. The cattle they brought to Texas in the late sixteenth century were hardy Spanish stock capable of thriving on cacti and going without water for long periods. The wild breed flourished in the Brush Country and developed into the fabled longhorn.

By the end of the Civil War six million branded and unbranded longhorns grazed the open ranges. A cow worth six to ten dollars in Texas sold for as much as forty dollars in the beef-hungry North. Though the markets were 1,500 to 2,000 miles away, the longhorns traveled well and gained weight on the trail. Generations on the open range developed the breed's long legs, exceptional strength, and wide horns.

For almost two decades, spring grass signaled the start of the drove on the Chisholm Trail, between the southern tip of Texas and Abilene, Kansas. By 1884, when the railroads and barbed wire ended the great trail drives, some ten million longhorns had been herded north.

Brush Country towns usually began as ranch headquarters with a company store,

saloon, and post office. Los Dos Laredos (the Two Laredos) was one town from the time of colonization in 1755 until 1848, when Mexico recognized the Rio Grande as Texas' border. Then residents had to make a choice: to remain Mexican citizens on the south bank or become Americans on the north. The decisions split families, but established a bond between the communities, which peaks each year with what is probably the country's most lavish celebration of George Washington's birthday. The observance began in 1897 when a group of civic leaders decided Laredo should commemorate a "purely American holiday." A highlight of the ten-day event is the Abrazo Ceremony, when the governors of Texas and the Mexican state of Nuevo León, and two schoolchildren from Laredo and Nuevo Laredo, meet in the middle of the International Bridge to exchange the traditional Spanish goodwill embrace.

The tangled landscape of Brush Country is a haven for white-winged dove, wild turkey, quail, white-tailed deer, and javelina. These animals lure hunters, including President Bush, to the area. South Texans call roadrunners, the comical birds that would rather skitter along the ground than fly, *paisanos*, or "fellow countrymen."

The region's largest city, Corpus Christi, developed around a half-moon bay with the same Latin name, meaning "body of Christ." The ambience here is more beach resort and sailboat center than cowboys and cattle. Instead of mesquite and cacti, Corpus sports palm trees and hibiscus. It is also the gateway to Padre Island National Seashore and an important deep water port.

© Steve Bentsen

RIGHT: *Sea oats rise above dunes that tides and winds constantly sculpt and change along the beaches of the Padre Island National Seashore.* INSET: *The green-backed heron nests in every region of Texas except the Llano Estacado.*

The Gulf Coast

Texans divide the state's 624 miles along the Gulf of Mexico into Galveston, South Padre, and "the Coast," a compact area that includes Port Aransas (Port A), Rockport/Fulton, and the Padre Island National Seashore.

The sandy, undeveloped reaches of the national seashore evoke an elusive ocean-wilderness mood. Tides and winds constantly sculpt the dunes, and sea oats sway gracefully above beige sand woven with purple railroad vine blossoms and patches of yellow evening primroses. The haunting cries of gulls, herons, and terns swooping

Wood Buffalo Refuge in Alberta to Texas. You don't have to be a birder to thrill at the sight of an ungainly whooper flapping its six- to seven-foot wingspan and soaring gracefully into the sky.

Port Aransas

"Port A" is the Cape Cod of the Lone Star State. The former fishing village on Mustang Island was accessible only by ferry until the 1950s. During the isolated years, the place had its own rules: liquor by the drink and gambling were legal on the Island even though the state of Texas didn't agree. Since the state didn't have boat patrols, officers had to use public transportation for

© Steve Bentsen

and sailing in the air currents pierce the surf's constant, wild pounding.

The grotesque shapes of stunted and slanted live oaks between Aransas Pass and Rockport are mute testimony to the gulf's forceful winds. The central flyway puts this area on the major migratory routes, and the bays and rookeries are ideal nesting spots that attract birders from all parts of the world.

In October the rare whooping cranes begin arriving from their Arctic nesting grounds in Canada to winter at the Aransas National Wildlife Refuge. Only fifteen of the endangered species remained when the refuge opened in 1937. In 1990, 146 made the 2,700-mile migration from

raids, and the ferries invariably developed motor problems on the way over. The green felt cloths and bars were gone by the time the Texas Rangers docked.

During the Depression, Port A residents saved money by pooling their resources annually to buy two sets of license plates. Anyone who had business on the mainland would put a set on the family car for the trip and turn the community property in upon return, so someone else could use the plates on their car.

It isn't apocryphal that Franklin D. Roosevelt escaped the pressures of the presidency at Port A, where he spent his days deep-sea fishing in the gulf and nights visiting with friends at the Tarpon Inn.

More than 500 miles of barrier islands off the mainland give Texas a double coastline along the Gulf of Mexico.

ABOVE: *Galveston is home port for the colorful shrimp fleet.*

Galveston

Galveston, about 230 miles east of Port Aransas, was the island home of the fierce Karankawa Indians, who smeared their bodies with bear grease to ward off mosquitoes and were said to be cannibalistic.

The French pirate Jean Laffite established the first settlement on the island and made it the operational base for his privateering and smuggling operations from 1817 to 1820.

Half a century later, Galveston became the world's leading cotton port. Banking and commerce flourished, and thousands of European emigrants touched Texas soil for the first time at Galveston.

A hurricane—still the worst natural disaster in American history—changed everything. More than 6,000 lives were lost

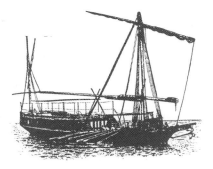

in the September 8, 1900, storm. The state's premier city was a shambles, although many stately mansions and iron-front buildings still were standing. The city was rebuilt ingeniously over the next decade; a 500-block area was elevated and provided with the protection of a ten-mile-long seawall. But by that time Houston, the aggressive neighbor fifty miles inland, had usurped Galveston's power position.

Houston

It's a wonder Houston ever happened, much less flourished into one of America's largest cities. The Allen brothers, a pair of wheeling, dealing New Yorkers, bought more than 6,000 acres of malaria- and yellow-fever-infested marshland on Buffalo Bayou in 1836 and named their trading post for General Sam Houston, who had become a hero by defeating the Mexican general Antonio López de Santa Anna at nearby San Jacinto four months earlier.

The Allens picked the site because flat-bottomed boats could take on goods at Galveston and move inland as far as the bayou, saving settlers fifty miles of arduous travel to the coast for supplies.

For years Houston maneuvered to make his namesake town the permanent capital, but he was thwarted by the people's preference for Austin's central loca-

BELOW: *Houston's dazzling skyline twinkles to life at sunset.*

tion. Frustrated on that political front, the city's developers decided to challenge Galveston's shipping monopoly by deepening and widening Buffalo Bayou in order to form the Houston Ship Channel.

The land dealt Houston's future a wild card in 1901, when the Oil Age exploded at the Spindletop oil field. Houston bankers rallied with financial backing for wildcatters and drilling companies. The flat, marshy land between Houston and the oil fields was perfect for the "Spaghetti Bowl," a network of pipelines connecting chemical plants, salt domes, processing plants, and refinery sites on the ship channel.

Successful gambling became Houston's hallmark. Space joined energy in 1961, when NASA accepted Rice University's offer of 1,000 acres twenty-five miles south of Houston as the site for the Manned Spacecraft Center—although there were mutterings that the choice was based more on then-vice president and native Texan Lyndon B. Johnson's role as chairman of the National Aeronautics and Space Council than on the land's merit. The city's link between earth and space echoed around the world with the first words spoken on the moon: "Houston...the Eagle has landed."

Innovative architecture is also a Houston trademark. In 1965 the Astrodome put sports under glass in air-conditioned, weather-free comfort. The city's reputation as a mecca for architectural innovation increased with each imaginative skyscraper sent soaring into the sky during the boom years. At night the Allen Brothers' trading post glitters and shimmers on the horizon like Oz.

OPPOSITE PAGE: *Rockets and other space memorabilia decorate the grounds of the Lyndon Baines Johnson Space Center like modernistic sculptures, giving the hub of America's space program a science-fiction setting.* **BELOW:** *Houston's Astrodome was dubbed the Eighth Wonder of the World when it opened on April 9, 1965. Astroturf was invented for the first all-weather stadium because grass wouldn't grow under glass.*

East Texas

The Piney Woods parallel the Louisiana border from just south of the Red River to the eastern edge of Houston. Spanish explorers considered the dense forests impenetrable, and Indians, filibusters, and other outlaws found refuge there among the bears, screaming panthers, and grunting wild hogs.

More than 400,000 acres of lakes weave through the wooded region. Most of the lakes are manmade, but Caddo Lake, in the upper corner, is the South's largest natural body of water. The relatively unspoiled aquatic paradise winds through towering cypress trees that are dripping with Spanish moss.

This continent's most diverse collection of plant life thrives in the Big Thicket, a biological crossroads that once was a flora and fauna wall covering 3.5 million acres within the Piney Woods until decades of development, particularly oil and timber exploitation, threatened extinction of the ecological belt.

The federal government eventually protected 84,500 scattered acres of the biological crossroads by creating the Big Thicket National Preserve. The area's native inhabitants included the Alabama-Coushatta Indians, whose descendants still live on land granted them by Sam Houston. At least two dozen wild orchid species are among the dense, marshy thicket's rare plant life.

For years oil was an agricultural curse. Farmers and ranchers dug wells, only to have badly needed water ruined by oil seepage. In 1866, a producing oil well was abandoned because there was no use for petroleum. Two decades later the Corsicana oil field led to the building of the state's first refinery, and the "oil bidness" went big time January 10, 1901, when Spindletop blew a gusher on the edge of the Piney Woods.

Beaumont, Orange, and Port Arthur—known as the Golden Triangle—became flourishing petroleum centers during the next decade, when the salt dome fields produced 42,773,650 barrels of oil. This drove land prices in the region up to 200,000 dollars an acre and oil prices down to three cents a barrel.

CENTER: *The loblolly gives the Piney Woods year-round verdancy and a delightful, fresh scent.* OPPOSITE PAGE: *Cypress trees have been guarding Texas' streams and lakes for centuries.*

~ Jefferson ~

The traditions and architectural legacies of the Old South linger throughout East Texas. By 1860, Jefferson was Texas' largest inland port, thanks to the Red River Raft, a natural dam of logs, silt, and debris that backed up the waters of Big Cypress Bayou, making it possible for steamboats to ply the waters between New Orleans and the East Texas town. River captains, merchants, and investors built impressive homes in Jefferson, and plantations dotted the surrounding countryside.

Jay Gould arrived in 1873 with plans for a railroad. When the city fathers turned down his request for right of way, the furious financier wrote a curse in the Excelsior House guest book: "The end of Jefferson."

No one took the threat seriously until the federal government ordered the Raft dynamited in order to facilitate navigation on the Red River. After a second blast, the waters of Big Cypress Bayou began to recede. By 1890, the former river port's population had dwindled from 30,000 to 2,000 people. Owners of the mansions moved on to other fortunes and many of the antebellum homes eventually were sold for back taxes.

More than half a century later, members of the Jessie Allen Wise Garden Club decided to revive the town's colorful past by sponsoring historic home tours. With the profits made from the pilgrimages, they bought the 1850 Excelsior House and rescued Jay Gould's private railroad car, named the Atalanta, from an ignominious life as a tenant house on an East Texas farm.

Dallas

Dallas is as uptown in most Texans' minds as Houston is upstart. "Big D" has class that transcends size.

Ever since John Neely Bryan, a Tennessee lawyer, located a trading post near a good fording spot on the Trinity River in 1841, Dallas has been a magnet for those willing to invest the necessary time and money to shape a first-rate city. The name Dallas honors a friend of Bryan's.

Initially, the fledgling populace placed the town on a wagon-trail route with an imposing name: Central National Highway of the Republic of Texas. Two decades later,

center—had a promising future, and attracted merchants and ambitious businessmen who founded banks and insurance companies there.

More than a century later, the wagon-trail route has been transformed into a mass merging of the interstate highway system, and the railroads have been upstaged by an international airport larger than the island of Manhattan.

The quest for class got a boost September 10, 1907, when Carrie Neiman and her brother, Herbert Marcus, founded "a new and exclusive shopping place for fashionable women." Long before "his-and-hers" gifts appeared in the 1960 Christmas catalog and an array of chic branch stores made Neiman-Marcus internationally famous,

OPPOSITE PAGE: This monumental bronze sculpture of nine larger-than-life mustangs charging down a stream is an impressive centerpiece for Williams Square at Las Colinas, a 12,000-acre development between downtown Dallas and the Dallas-Fort Worth International Airport. INSET: Modern skyscrapers in downtown Dallas. BELOW: The ranch gate recognized throughout the world.

© Courtesy of Texas Highways Magazine

an important railroad intersection seemed destined to miss Dallas by twenty miles. Citizens mustered their wits and money with a land-subsidy offer fortified by a clause requiring the railroad's crosspoint to be no more than a mile from Browder Springs. The bill became law before rival communities discovered that the springs were the source of Dallas' water supply.

As the hub of two rail lines, Dallas quickly became the Southwest's leading distribution center and Texas' largest city. The burgeoning metropolis—which was a thriving cotton market in the 1870s and later developed into a financial and cultural

Texans embraced the Neiman's at Main and Ervay, the flagship store identified only by the small brass plates that were located on the cornerstones.

The city's name spans the globe via the rise and fall of "America's Team," the Dallas Cowboys, and the escapades of the Ewing family on the long-running television series *Dallas*. The primetime soap opera may have faded from the screen, but Southfork and J.R. will remain immortal.

BELOW: *Big Tex has been greeting fairgoers for four decades.* OPPOSITE PAGE: *Beautifully preserved nineteenth-century buildings make downtown Fort Worth an interesting mixture of the city's past and present.*

A LONE STAR ~ STATEMENT ~

Air-conditioning corralled the heat and humidity, and the plane defeated distances for Texans. In 1970, Southwest became "the national airline of Texas," with flights linking the state like jet-propelled pogo sticks. To celebrate the airline's twentieth birthday in 1990, Herb Kelleher, Southwest's maverick president, had Boeing paint a 737 like the Lone Star flag. The distinctive red, white, and blue plane is used only for flights within Texas.

Fort Worth

Dallas' neighbor, Fort Worth, is as western in styles and origins as Dallas is eastern. Established as an army camp in 1849, its location on the edge of the Chisholm Trail, a cattle-driving route cut in 1867, and the Trinity River bottom made Fort Worth a popular resting and replenishing spot. Cowboys were ready for fun when they reached "Cowtown," as the place became known. They found diversion in Hell's Half Acre, six blocks of saloons and bawdy houses where drovers could get "a drink, a girl, and a poker game" any time of the day or night.

When the trail drives ended in 1884, Fort Worth built stockyards and got rail connections that enabled Cowtown to become one of the world's greatest cattle markets. Fort Worth is still "Where the West Begins," with strong cultural infusions from the Kimbell Art Museum, Amon Carter Museum of Western Art, and Fort Worth Art Center.

~ BIG TEX ~

He wears a seventy-five gallon hat and size seventy boots. His custom-made jeans have a twenty-six waist and twenty-seven and a half inseam—that's feet, not inches. Big Tex has been looming over the entrance to the State Fair of Texas in Dallas since 1952. Over the years he's gained a voice and animation and grown from forty-seven to fifty-two feet. Like the Art Deco buildings in Fair Park that are a legacy of the 1936 Texas Centennial and the Texas-Oklahoma football classic, Big Tex is a fixture of the country's largest state fair.

© Robert Lima/Envision

Panhandle Plains

The Panhandle Plains includes the area from the New Mexico border, southwest of Lubbock, to the northernmost boundary along the Texas and Oklahoma panhandles. Sixteenth-century Spanish maps

identified most of the land as the Llano Estacado, or Staked Plains, a name probably derived from the explorers' need to stake routes across the vast grasslands to guide them back to Mexico.

For centuries no trees broke the horizon-to-horizon landscape. The grasses nurtured millions of buffalo that fulfilled the needs of the Comanche who made the High Plains their domain. Development eventually destroyed the great grasslands, and settlers planted trees.

Twenty-two miles south of Amarillo, the flat, gray-beige land splits into a 120-mile-long, multicolored canyon that is the Caprock Escarpment's most dramatic surface feature. In its most scenic areas, Palo Duro Canyon is almost two miles wide, with bluffs rising 1,200 feet from the floor. Geologists say a series of rivers and creeks cut

When Texas needed a new Capitol in 1880, land was its only tangible asset. The constitution earmarked three million acres stretching across ten Panhandle Plains counties to finance construction. The Capitol Syndicate, a group of Chicago entrepreneurs who successfully bid on the project, ended up paying one dollar and seven cents an acre for the ranch they called the XIT. The world's largest fenced operation had seven division headquarters within boundaries ranging 200 miles north to south and twenty-seven miles east to west. It also had more than 500 windmills, the invention that changed farming and ranching by diminishing dependence on surface water. Around 1900, the Capitol Syndicate began selling off the XIT, and by 1912 all that remained was the ranch's famous three-letter brand.

Like asphalt ribbons, twin highways roll across the Panhandle.

© Steven Bentsen

through the earth en route to the ocean. Aided by fierce winds, the waters carved deeper and deeper and the walls took on ledges and cross beds ribboned with vivid earth tones. Palo Duro, Spanish for hardwood, is a reference to the juniper trees growing in the canyon. Indians used to make them into arrows. Springs and plant life made the canyon a refuge for conquistadors and settlers as well as tribes.

After the 1874 defeat of the last Comanche and Kiowa tribes in Palo Duro Canyon, huge ranches developed across the Panhandle Plains. Palo Duro Canyon became part of the J.A., founded by John Adair and Charles Goodnight, who designed the first chuck wagon, a rolling galley with compartments for staples and cooking utensils. The Matador, Frying Pan, and Three D, a cattle and oil kingdom that

© Courtesy of Texas Highways Magazine

made the Waggoners one of Texas' wealthiest families, never matched the XIT's size, but each covers thousands of acres.

Amarillo and Lubbock

Amarillo—the buffalo trading post that became the hub of the High Plains—is located nearer to the capital cities of Colorado, New Mexico, and Oklahoma than it is to Austin. Yet people in this region are distinctively Texan. Cowboys seen on the streets still round up cattle, although they probably use four-wheel-drive trucks or "whirly-herd" with helicopters.

Amarillo means yellow in Spanish, but the pronunciation is Texan, so don't pronounce the "ll" as a "y," as Spanish-speaking people do.

One hundred twenty miles to the south, Lubbock rises above the plains like a mirage. Instead of pastures rolling with tumbleweed, grain, cotton, and vineyards fill the surrounding fields. Irrigation systems constantly click, compensating for the lack of annual rainfall that kept the area from developing its agricultural potential until after World War II.

THE CADILLAC OF ~ SCULPTURE ~

Just outside Amarillo, ten vintage Cadillacs, circa 1949 to 1963, have been planted hoods-down, fins-up in cement at the edge of a wheatfield. Graffiti covers the bodies and tail decorations of the bizarre artwork, which was commissioned by Stanley Marsh Three, a millionaire noted for eccentric projects and pranks who lives nearby on his ranch, Toad Hall.

A crop of Cadillacs edges wheatfields outside Amarillo.

Hill Country/Highland Lakes

The Balcones Escarpment, a long fault line extending from the Rio Grande to the Red River, is scarcely discernible in most areas, but in Central Texas the geological uplift becomes highly visible in the Edwards Plateau, commonly called the Hill Country. The

rough grass. In the spring bluebonnets, Indian paintbrush, pink primroses, and other vivid wildflowers blanket the fields.

Beneath the fault line, a network of caves extends from Central Texas to far West Texas. Fantastic, delicately colored formations created by water dripping for millennia through the porous rock decorate the caverns.

On the edge of the Hill Country, softly rolling wooded hills and sparkling waters surround Austin—Texas' capital city in every sense of the word. Houston has San

© Susan Gibler

OPPOSITE PAGE: *The Hill Country's spring-fed streams are ideal cooling-off spots in the summer.* **LEFT:** *Spring wildflower displays featuring the pale pink primrose, bluebonnet, and orange-red Indian paintbrush attract visitors from all parts of the world to the Texas Hill Country.*

blacklands, a fertile dark-soil prairie, lie east of the fault line; to the west, limestone-based rock is never far from the surface.

Spanish explorers called the cliffs along the edge of the plateau *balcones*, because the limestone walls framing the rivers appeared to have balconies. The escarpment also served as a natural fence for buffalo herds, since the animals' instincts kept them in cooler climates above the fault line.

Ancient cypresses, transplanted from the trees' swamp habitats by migratory birds, shade clear, cold streams fed by springs bubbling out of the honeycomb rock. The soft, rolling terrain belies the Hill Country's hardscrabble nature. Native junipers, which Texans call "cedars," stand beside twisted mesquite and oaks in pastures where goats and sheep graze on

Jacinto, San Antonio has the Alamo, and Dallas has Southfork, but Austin is the only one that has the Capitol.

Soon after his election as the second president of the republic in 1838, Mirabeau B. Lamar and a group of buffalo-hunting friends camped near Waterloo, a four-family settlement on the Colorado River. The area's attractions prompted Lamar to write an eloquent recommendation to the commission he'd named to select a permanent capital site.

Within weeks the committee proposed that the Texas Congress approve the location, adding that it was "worthy only of being the home of the brave and the free." The lawmakers concurred and stipulated that the capital's name must honor the "Father of Texas," Stephen F. Austin.

ABOVE: *The noon Sunday mariachi mass celebration at Mission San Jose in San Antonio continues in the mission courtyard after the service.* **OPPOSITE PAGE:** *The Goddess of Liberty topped the Capitol dome from 1888 until 1985, when her hollow, zinc body began to show the lady's age. This replica, cast in molds made from the original statue and named Goddess of Liberty II, assumed the honored position with the help of a Skycrane helicopter on June 14, 1986.*

Edwin Waller, a signer of the Texas Declaration of Independence, drew up a town plan centered on a wide thoroughfare sweeping from the river to Capitol Hill. Congress Avenue, crowned by the stately pink granite Capitol, is still the heart of downtown Austin.

The city's appeal doesn't hinge solely on its role as the state's political power center. Austin's allure is rooted in natural beauty and a relaxed charm that make it every Texan's heart-of-heart hometown. More than 47,000 students on the University of Texas' main campus give the population a decidedly youthful flavor.

Seven Highland Lakes, created by dams on the Colorado River, begin 100 miles northwest of the city at Lake Buchanan and twist through the countryside to Town Lake, at the foot of Congress Avenue. The banning of motorized boats make the lakes a mecca for sculls and canoes. Native trees and flowers line eight miles of hiking and biking trails along the shoreline, made possible by an ambitious landscaping project spurred by Lady Bird Johnson, who main-

AUSTIN'S WINGED ~ PROGENY ~

From March through October the Congress Avenue Bridge is home to North America's largest urban bat colony. About a million pregnant Mexican free-tailed bats migrate to Austin in the spring, and each gives birth to a single pup in June. Austinites gather on the banks of Town Lake to watch the mammals swirl up from under the bridge at dusk to begin their hunt for insects. The show goes on hold in the autumn, when mothers and their young rejoin the colony of males south of the border.

tains an Austin home in addition to the LBJ Ranch located at nearby Stonewall, the late president's Hill Country birthplace.

THAT PINK CAPITOL

What's a macho state doing with a pink Capitol?

Original plans called for the statehouse to be a creamy white, native limestone copy of the national Capitol, but when construction began in 1886 the architect discovered there wasn't enough top-quality stone available. Owners of Granite Mountain, fifty-five miles from Austin, offered to donate 15,000 carloads of pink granite from their quarry in exchange for a railroad link to the capital city, a deal that the cash-strapped state couldn't turn down. As a result, the entire Capitol complex is rosy. But there is a Texas touch: the distinctive, 309-foot dome rises seven feet higher than its Washington, D.C., counterpart.

San Antonio

Sure as Austin is the place most Texans would like to live, San Antonio is their favorite vacation spot. You'll never confuse it with any other American city. It's a domestic destination with a Mexican flavor.

The city got its start when Spanish explorers established a halfway post on the banks of the San Antonio River in 1718 to break the distance between the East Texas missions and their northernmost garrison in Coahuila, Mexico. The post, Presidio de Bejar, eventually had a companion mission, called San Antonio de Valero, that gained immortality in 1836 as the Alamo. The route they charted later became El Camino Real, the Royal Road.

The Franciscans established four more successful missions along the river, and in 1731, fifteen Canary Island families became Texas' first European settlers. La Villita, the "little village" where the Canary Islanders lived, and the restored missions are among the preserved structures that so beautifully blend yesterday's patina into the modern sparkle and glitter of America's ninth largest city.

⌒ THE RIVER WALK ⌒

Romantic Paseo del Rio, the River Walk, is one magnificent feature that sets San Antonio apart. The meandering stream, situated a level below the city's bustling commercial center, has an enchanting Brigadoon quality.

During the day, pedestrians strolling along flower-bordered paths exchange greetings with passengers floating by on brightly colored barges. Sunshine shimmers through towering cypress trees that line the banks and shade diners at sidewalk cafés. Hand-holding couples dawdle from shop to shop, and crowd-watchers nibble nachos and sip cool drinks at umbrella-shaded tables.

With sunset the River Walk shifts into an after-dark mood. The tinkle of glassware, silver, and china replaces the chirping of birds, and twinkling lights dapple the water. Tour barges become party boats, and the brassy strains of mariachis fill the air.

From the Friday after Thanksgiving through New Year's Day, thousands of tiny lights outline the trees and graceful stone bridges of the River Walk. On December weekends, choirs serenade from barges, and lumina-rias cast a soft glow along the banks. Las Posadas, a reenactment of the Holy Family's search for shelter, highlights the Christmas celebration.

Harmless dyes turn the tributary green for St. Patrick's Day, and the stream becomes a floating parade route during Fiesta San Antonio, a festival that began in 1891 as a tribute to the Texians' victory at San Jacinto. Dates for the ten-day celebration always include April 21, the anniversary of that 1836 battle.

The picturesque landmark would have been a U-shaped storm sewer if it hadn't been for a dedicated group of preservationists. After a disastrous 1921 flood claimed fifty lives and caused millions of dollars in damage, engineers recommended the elimination of the horseshoe curve through the business district and conversion of the abandoned riverbed into a paved drainage ditch topped with a street. Civic groups, led by the San Antonio Conservation Society, stymied the project and came up with an alternate plan that cuts the horseshoe bend off from the mainstream with two weir dams during floods.

OPPOSITE PAGE: *Although San Antonio's River Walk is several miles in length, it can be walked in a little over an hour—but it shouldn't be. The mood along this landscaped, cypress-shaded walk, with its unique shops, galleries, and cafés, is as relaxed as the river—so take enough time to enjoy it.* **RIGHT:** *The River Walk during the evening.*

Chapter Two

THE PEOPLE

Being a native is a birthright most Texans take considerably more pride in than outsiders deem necessary. In these days of homogenized cultures, there are those who say such provincial roots, which are often only one or two generations deep, are irrelevant.

If that's so, why does George Bush think it's important to claim to be a Texan? And why did Lyndon Johnson believe being one was imperative?

Any time Texans bother to debate President Bush's dearth of bona fide Lone Star credentials, someone invariably comes to place the blame squarely where it belongs: "His momma and poppa should have planned ahead."

If you follow that line of genealogical reasoning, perhaps it *is* absurd that Texans feel conceit about where they were fortunate enough to be born—since merely showing up provided us with bragging rights. But I do admit to deriving a chauvinistic arrogance from the fact that my grandparents, like thousands of other Europeans, chose to emigrate directly to Texas from Denmark and Germany.

I don't know that I've ever encountered anyone who regretted being born a Texan, although quite a few transplants to the state have been known to disdain the place, right down to the cockroaches and armadillos—not to mention rattlesnakes and 100-degree summers.

More than a decade before the rest of America got caught up in the *Roots* syndrome, Texas began exploring its ethnic beginnings. The Institute of Texan Cultures opened in 1968 as the state's pavilion at HemisFair, San Antonio's 250th birthday celebration. The original exhibits and multimedia displays traced the contributions twenty-one ethnic groups made to the early history of Texas, but the scope since has expanded to include twenty-six nationalities that are part of the Texan heritage. Research continues to add new chapters to the saga.

Every August the grounds surrounding the Institute of Texan Cultures showcase an ethnic extravaganza. The four-day Texas Folklife Festival celebrates the music, folk dances, arts, crafts, and foods of the varied cultures that are Texans' rootstock. Polkas and kolaches, mariachis and tamales, schottisches and wurst, zydeco and jambalaya, blues and hush puppies, country-western and barbecue are only a sampling of the blended diversities that help to make Texas special.

Back in the seventies, when New York was the only gateway to Europe for flying Texans, I returned from foreign assignments with great anticipation of the homecoming joy awaiting me in the Braniff lounges at J.F.K. or LaGuardia airports. It was comforting to hear other Texans drawling and twanging about their adventures in Rome, London, or "Parisfrance" and debating whether they hungered most for Tex-Mex, barbecue, or chicken-fried steak. There was an encompassing camaraderie among strangers because we were all Texans "goin' home."

Institute of Texan Cultures

ABOVE: *This Caddo Indian town, as depicted in George Nelson's mural, is based on the Caddoan Mounds State Historic Site. Around A.D. 1100, the site was a town of several thousand people, with artificial mounds built for burials of the elite members of the society and for temples. Pages 44-45: The Southwest Indian look is fashionable today.*

Today, with flights available to all parts of the world from the Dallas/Fort Worth and Houston airports, my seatmate these days is more likely to be a Korean computer whiz, a Vietnamese restaurateur, or a sari-clad young woman from Bombay who is en route to help her husband with the management of their West Texas motel. It is their children who will be the next generation of native Texans.

When asked why he made the decision to use Texas as the subject for one of his epic novels, James Michener replied with the highly illuminating statement, "Texas has a reverberating quality that other

places don't have: Its diverse history pulls on the imagination."

That "reverberating quality" has given us Texans a reputation for marching to a different drummer, or perhaps, more accurately, to our own drum and bugle corps. The "diverse history" has woven a Texas mystique and kindled a sense of self-sufficiency we think is unique to the Lone Star State.

Every year on March 2, Texans around the world repeat this toast to commemorate the anniversary of the 1836 Declaration of Independence that created the Republic of Texas.

The Indians

It was the Indians who originally gave the state of Texas its name. When the first Franciscan padres arrived to establish missions in the territory the Spanish called "New Philippines," they found the Caddo farming and living in permanent structures located among the piney woods along what was France's Louisiana border.

The tribe described themselves as "Tay-shas," or friends and allies. After some debate about the spelling, the government decreed that Spain's land north of Mexico

A FATEFUL ~ ENCOUNTER ~

One of the Indian Wars' most poignant stories involves Cynthia Ann Parker, a nine-year-old girl taken prisoner when a Comanche tribe raided her family compound at Fort Parker. Twenty-four years later, Texas Rangers found a blue-eyed squaw called Naduah among prisoners taken during a tribal raid. When she responded to her real name, elated relatives took Cynthia Ann and her young daughter, Prairie Flower, to live with them. But she couldn't adjust to their way of life and tried to escape for four years, begging to rejoin her husband, Chief Peta Nocona, and her sons. Six months after Prairie Flower's death, Cynthia Ann died at age thirty-seven. Her son Quanah was elected the last great Comanche chief and represented the tribe during negotiations in Washington, D.C.

would be known as Tejas, which eventually became Texas. Early colonists called themselves Texians, and for a reason no longer known, Texians became Texans with the arrival of statehood.

Before the Spaniards introduced livestock to the Southwest in the sixteenth century, the nomadic tribes traveled only as far as their feet could carry them. Since buffalo supplied the Indians' needs, they weren't too interested in the imported cattle and pigs, but the mustangs put the tribes on horseback and changed history. The Apache and Comanche quickly mastered riding and light cavalry skills. For almost three centuries *mestenos*—the small, hardy, wild offspring of the conquistadors' mustangs—gave the tribes freedom to roam and strike at enemies with terrifying quickness.

In the end, dependence on the horse led to the Indians' defeat. The final chapter of the Texas Indian Campaign unfolded in Palo Duro Canyon, September 29, 1874, when the last tribes surrendered after federal troops destroyed their horse herds.

© Robert Lima/Envision

Missions

"When the ministers are not watching, the Indians go off into the woods and there hold their dances," the eighteenth-century Franciscan missionary Father José de Solis wrote in his diary.

The missions were much more than churches. Along with their religious convictions, the padres brought European farm implements and tools, agricultural and engineering skills, grains, seeds, and cuttings for vineyards. Each mission was a self-sustaining village with living quarters, workshops, a church, and an acequia to provide irrigation. Within the walls, Indians learned weaving, milling, construction, farming, and ranching. The Karankawa and other hostile tribes were poor candidates for conversion, but the new way of life saved docile tribes, such as the Coahuiltecan, from extinction at the hands of their warring counterparts, although many died in epidemics of relatively minor European illnesses.

Descendants of the Indians who received land allotments after secularization in 1794 still live around the San Antonio missions, and a sense of community continues at the historic sites, since all four are active parishes. The mariachi mass Sunday at noon in Mission San Jose is a joyous celebration of life.

The Empresarios

After a period of benign neglect, the Spaniards decided to use the *empresario* system in order to colonize Texas. Under the plan, a leader, called an *empresario,* received a large land grant for bringing in permanent settlers, all of whom received cheap or free acreage. This system brought an influx of Mexican settlers, who established rancheros in South Texas.

After Mexico won independence from Spain in 1820, the system continued with the stipulation that *empresarios* and their colonists must be Catholic. At the time, the English Penal Codes prohibited Catholics from owning land, so Ireland became a wellspring for *empresarios* and settlers, who founded the Brush Country ranches that still remain under family ownership.

OPPOSITE PAGE: *The Apache traveled through Texas following the great herds of buffalo. This photograph shows an Apache mother with baby bound to her back in a wicker basket ready for travel.* **ABOVE:** *Historic battles involving the Spaniards, Indians, Mexicans, and Anglo settlers were fought through the years at La Bahia. After their defeat at Coleta, James Fannin and his Texian troops were imprisoned in the presidio chapel for a week before being massacred by Mexican forces.*

FPG International

Anglo-Americans

In 1822, Stephen F. Austin brought in 300 Anglo-American families, still known as the Old 300, who prospered on rich bottomland farms along the Colorado and Brazos rivers. Only eight months after the territory Austin opened to Anglo-American settlement became a republic, the "Father of Texas" died a bachelor at age forty-seven.

Word of the families' success sparked an exodus among farmers trying to eke out a living on burned-out farmland throughout the American South and Midwest. "GTT"—short for Gone to Texas—became the graffiti byword on abandoned tenant cabins from Missouri to Tennessee. Anyone wanting to make a fresh start headed for Texas.

Cultural, religious, political, and language differences between the American settlers and the Mexican bureaucracy mushroomed, compounding the threat of tribal attacks, disease, harsh weather, and the labor and frustration it took to cultivate and tame a wilderness. Most of all, the Americans' ideas of justice and political freedom bore no resemblance to the rules laid down by Mexico's dictator-president, Antonio López de Santa Anna, who ruled sporadically from 1824 to 1855 and often shifted party allegiances.

Unrest and increasing skirmishes with Mexican troops and officials attracted a new genre of Americans who had grown up hearing their grandfathers and fathers spin heroic tales of the American Revolution and War of 1812. Some were idealists, others were hotheads and professional scrappers looking for a fight. All called themselves Texians.

Revolution

Unrest and violence flamed and faded in Texas for a decade before Santa Anna decided to personally quell the revolt by retaking San Antonio in 1836.

Even though it was a tragic, lost cause, the price paid by 189 patriots who died at the Alamo fired the freedom spirit among Texians. Whether the stories surrounding the epic, thirteen-day siege are true or apocryphal really isn't important. The spirit was there: defend until death.

On March 2, 1836, delegates meeting at Washington-on-the-Brazos signed the Declaration of Independence and elected Sam Houston commander-in-chief of the Texas Army. Four days later the Alamo fell.

Santa Anna fanned the rebels' rage to fury three weeks later by ordering the execution of 342 Texians imprisoned at La Bahia Presidio in Goliad.

Assuming the revolt was over, Santa Anna eventually marched 1,600 of his men south, and set up camp near Buffalo Bayou. According to legend, when Houston's ragtag army attacked on April 21, Emily Morgan, a beautiful mulatto slave, was entertaining the general while his men took their afternoon siesta. Shouting "Remember the Alamo! Remember Goliad!", the Texians won the battle in eighteen minutes. Houston was wounded, Santa Anna was captured, and Emily Morgan was immortalized in the song, "Yellow Rose of Texas."

OPPOSITE PAGE: *Moses Austin died less than three months after receiving an empresario grant from Mexico; his son, Stephen Fuller Austin, assumed the task of bringing the first Anglo-American settlers into Texas in 1822. Despite being imprisoned in Mexico City for more than two years as a result of his efforts to achieve reforms, Austin remained a fervent loyalist until 1835. After losing the first presidential election in 1836, he became the new republic's secretary of state.* **LEFT:** *The Alamo in the center of downtown San Antonio is Texas' Shrine of Liberty.*

© Marc Fort

～ JUNETEENTH ～

Juneteenth, Texas' own commemoration of the Emancipation Proclamation, dates to June 19, 1865, when Major General Gordon Granger sailed into Galveston and announced that slaves had been free since January 1, 1863. Parades, barbecues, and dances highlight the annual festivities. For years the holiday also signaled the opening of outdoor stands selling watermelon by the slice, because blacks and whites alike firmly believed it was unhealthy to eat the fruit before Juneteenth.

Juneteenth—the commemoration of Major General Gordon Granger's landing in Galveston on June 19, 1865, and his announcement that all slaves were free—is a holiday unique to Texas. Juneteenth is celebrated throughout the state with parades and picnics.

The Europeans

Visions of unlimited cheap land and freedom in the new republic blinded oppressed Europeans to the harsh realities of frontier life. Going to Texas sounded like a trip to paradise.

More than 7,000 Germans eagerly paid 240 dollars for a family package covering transportation to Texas, 320 acres of land, a log house, and financing through the first year's crop. Poles, Moravians, Bohemians, Wends, Norwegians, Swedes, Danes, and Alsatians accepted similar offers.

Shipboard epidemics claimed many during the arduous voyages, which lasted two to three months. Unscrupulous speculators often failed to provide transportation for the long trips from the coast to their land, and since the newcomers had no money, walking was their only option. Some contracted yellow fever, cholera, and malaria before leaving Galveston or Indianola, the Texas ports of entry. Graves of newborn babies and their mothers, and victims of weather and disease marked the trails leading inland.

Those who survived took in orphaned children and set about conquering the strange new land. Unlike their American counterparts who traded one frontier for another, the Europeans brought memories of majestic cathedrals, castles, and centuries-old cities along with their languages and cultures. Dissatisfied with log-cabin living, they quickly set about building permanent stone structures that give many Texas communities their old-world charm.

Buffalo Soldiers

In one of history's ironic twists, black troopers opened vast areas to white settlement by driving the Indians out of West Texas after the Civil War.

The Comanche, Kiowa, and Apache called men of the Ninth and Tenth Cavalry "Buffalo Soldiers," because their hair reminded the Indians of the bison's curly, woolly coat. The nickname also was given as a tribute to the troops' stamina and perseverance, since the poorly equipped units rode thousands of miles through relentless terrain and punishing weather pursuing the elusive tribes, building new roads, stringing telegraph wires, and charting wilderness.

Most of the Buffalo Soldiers were freedmen without homes, jobs, or education who volunteered in return for food, shelter, clothing, and thirteen dollars a month. They also got automatic assignment to hazardous-duty forts scattered across the barren Texas frontier, plus cast-off uniforms and equipment, harsh double-standard conduct codes, and scorn from the settlers they protected.

White officers received promotions as reward for accepting duty with the all-black enlisted units, but the assignment of West Point's first black graduate to the Tenth Cavalry at Fort Concho in San Angelo turned out to be tragic typecasting. Even though Lieutenant Henry O. Flipper had an outstanding military record, he was court-martialed and dishonorably discharged in 1882 for "conduct unbecoming an officer," a charge trumped up after he was seen riding with a young white woman. The army didn't right the blatant wrong until 1976, thirty-six years after Flipper's death.

For decades the only recognition of the Buffalo Soldiers' bravery and distinguished service was their Indian adversaries' badge of honor, the buffalo emblem they proudly wore on their uniform sleeves.

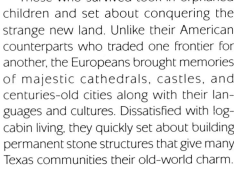

Texas Music

Saturday's magic lingers in Texas. That was the day the predominantly rural population went into town to shop, visit, and dance.

Fiddlers were as indispensable as a rifle in early Texas. The self-taught musicians sawed out tunes that helped settlers forget the cares of pioneer life as they do-si-doed and waltzed.

Texas' geographic position between the South, the West, and Mexico—combined with European infusions—led to the development of distinctive musical styles.

The slaves' mournful, "work-holler" field laments and joyous gospel messages, cowboys' work songs, and Mexicans' ballads eventually blended together. Czechs and Poles added polka rhythms and the accordion, and German brass bands contributed oompah-pah.

Blind Lemon Jefferson, Huddie (Leadbelly) Ledbetter, Mance Lipscomb, and Lightnin' Sam Hopkins are talents most associated with early blues, particularly in Dallas' Deep Ellum district. Many years after Scott Joplin honed ragtime, Stevie Ray Vaughan and the Fabulous Thunderbirds would redefine rhythm and blues.

Still, country-western is most typically Texan. The musical sound sets feet to dancing the Texas two-step and cotton-eyed Joe. It is the perfect background for honky-tonks and dance halls.

Bob Wills and the Texas Playboys did more to perpetuate the popularity of country-western music than any other group. Wills took a page from the big band sound of the 1930s and combined western with swing. The first notes of his classic "San Antonio Rose" evoke a spontaneous "EEEEEE-HA" from Texans.

Ernest Tubbs was one of the first country-western balladeers to add the electric guitar's punch to his woeful musical tales of broken dreams, heartless women, and sleepless nights—country-western's favorite themes.

Willie Nelson, Waylon Jennings, Jerry Jeff Walker, Ray Price, George Jones, and George Strait continue the state's tradition of country-western talent that began when Gene Autry and Tex Ritter sang their way to the movie screen and made "Home on the Range" the cowhands' theme song.

By peppering their style and songs with a bit of Cajun zydeco and a lot of Tex-Mex *conjunto,* current headliners have given country-western the full Lone Star flavor that makes Saturday night dancing so much fun.

Texas Rangers

Mired in debt, the new republic couldn't finance an army to control Mexican invasions, tribal attacks, and lawlessness, so the Texas Congress commissioned a militia to keep order. Initially, the mounted gunmen didn't have a name, but they soon became known as the Texas Rangers.

RIGHT: *The exploits of the celebrated lawmen who brought order to all parts of the state are showcased in Waco's Texas Ranger Museum.*

Courtesy of Texas Rangers Hall of Fame

Jack Hays, Ben McCulloch, W.A.A. "Big Foot" Wallace, and Samuel H. Walker were among the first Rangers who fought and thought like their enemies, the Indians and the Mexicans. Walter Prescott Webb, the renowned historian, wrote that a Ranger could "ride like a Mexican, trail like an Indian, shoot like a Tennessean, and fight like the devil."

Some called them "commissioned cowboys," because they had no permanent stations or uniforms, and most of the colorful characters wore custom-crafted boots, beaver fur Stetsons, and heavy silver belt buckles. They also made the deadly Colt revolver their hallmark weapon and suggested improvements that were readily adopted by the inventor, Samuel Colt.

The Rangers served as scouts for federal troops during the Mexican War and led raiding parties across the border. Their intervention settled land disputes and bitter family feuds. During Reconstruction's chaos, the Rangers tracked down Sam Bass, John Wesley Hardin, and other desperadoes. Their successors ended Bonnie and Clyde's terror reign in the 1930s.

A 1919 investigation exposed vigilante actions by Rangers patrolling the Mexican border, so the legislature ordered the force's strength reduced from more than a thousand to seventy-five men, a tradition that continues.

A popular Texas saying, "One riot, one Ranger," stems from the time a sheriff called headquarters begging for backup to quell a riot. A few hours later, a Ranger arrived.

"They only sent one Ranger?" the astonished sheriff asked.

"You got more than one riot?" the Ranger shot back.

Cowboys and the Rodeo

The legendary Texas cowboy got his training and his trappings from the Mexican *vaquero,* who designed a saddle he could stay astride during roundups and stampedes and wore a sombrero to ward off the relentless sun and rain. Heavy canvas pants, leather chaps, and boots provide protection from thorns, brush, and snakes, and a bandanna catches the range's choking dust. Corral, rancho, loco, and bronco are among the *vaquero* words that passed into cowboy culture.

Roundups, originally called by the Spanish word *rodeo,* spurred riding and roping competitions among the cowboys. The contests became a form of recreation to break the monotony of the long periods spent on the range and trail drives, and eventually cowhands from neighboring ranches contended for prizes during rodeos staged to highlight holiday celebrations. Mexican *vaqueros* called similar contests *charreadas* and the cowboys who competed *charros.*

Bill Pickett, the first black man enshrined in the Rodeo Hall of the National Cowboy Hall of Fame, traveled around the world exhibiting bulldogging skills he honed as a Central Texas range rider in the late nineteenth century. Pickett's specialty was "nose-biting," a variation on bulldogging that involved grabbing the steer's horns and twisting its neck so he could bite the animal's tender upper lip and force the steer to the ground.

Calf roping; bareback, saddle bronco, and bull riding; barrel racing; and steer wrestling, as bulldogging now is known, are among the feature events on the rodeo circuit, which kicks off in January at the Southwestern Exposition and Livestock Show in Fort Worth, where the first indoor rodeo was staged in 1917. Professionals compete for prizes and for points that count toward the naming of national champion

Indoor and outdoor rodeos throughout the state draw huge crowds and skilled professional competitors.

cowboys and cowgirls at the end of the rodeo season.

Show biz is very much a part of today's rodeos. Major Texas cities, with the notable exception of Dallas, host 10-day rodeos in conjunction with livestock shows and performances of country-western stars. During the summer months, hundreds of small towns across Texas stage rodeo weekends.

By the way, the word is pronounced ROW-dee-oh, not ro-DAY-oh, as Californians familiar with the famous shopping street Rodeo Drive might say.

Talkin' Texan

Just as there is no typical Texan, there is no universal identifying accent: East Texans talk with a drawl; West Texans' speech tends to twang; North and Central Texans generally drawl *and* twang; while South Texans spice their accent with Spanish words and phrases.

FPG International

OPPOSITE PAGE: *The ten-gallon hat and a lariat, traditional Texas cowboy trappings borrowed from their Mexican counterparts.* **LEFT:** *Because Samuel Colt had trouble marketing his revolver in the East, he brought his invention to Texas, where it was given the name 'six-shooter.' Today's pistol evolved from Colt's original.*

Texans tend to sprinkle colorful clichés throughout their speech like conversational confetti, and delight in provincial pronunciations that put a Lone Star brand on the English language.

Not everyone shares our enthusiasm, however. International journalists covering Lyndon Johnson's stays at his ranch, or "Texas White House," on the Pedernales River were taken aback when LBJ and his native constituents referred to the river as the "Perd'n-alice."

By the same reasoning, or lack of it, Bexar, as in Bexar County, is pronounced "bear." Buchanan, as in Lake Buchanan, is BUCK-hanan, because that's the way Senator Buchanan pronounced his family name, and the first of the Highland Lakes honors his memory. Manchacha is MAN-shack; Burnet is BURN-it, and Elgin, a Central Texas town where they make famous sausage, not watches, rhymes with "ben."

THE FIRST ~ MAVERICK ~

Samuel Augustus Maverick, a Yale graduate from South Carolina who joined the Texian cause and was one of the signers of the republic's Declaration of Independence, gave his name to the English language because he was too busy serving in the legislature to bother with branding his free-roaming cattle. At roundup time the neighbors would sort out the herds and earmark unbranded cattle as "one of Maverick's." Eventually, maverick came to mean unbranded stock, and today a maverick is anyone who thinks and acts independently. That definition aptly describes Samuel's grandson, Maury, a politician and attorney who was a defender of civil liberties long before the passage of the Civil Rights Act.

A TEXAN LEXICON

Dance With the Guy Who Brung You: *Don't change a thing.*

Fixin' to: *Getting ready to do something: "Are yawl fixin' to go to town?" Note that the "g" in the present participle "ing" is silent in Texas.*

A Fur Piece: *Great distance. "It's a fur piece from Amarillo to Brownsville."*

He'd Wear a Sam Browne Belt and Suspenders With Overalls: *Too cautious to be a Texan.*

High Cotton: *The top of the heap.*

A Hoot and a Holler: *Someone who is good at kickin' up his or her heels, as in "Bubba is a hoot and a holler." Also the opposite of "fur piece" in describing distances: "Round Rock is just a hoot and a holler from Austin."*

Hotter Than a Two-Dollar Pistol: *Anything or anybody that's on a roll.*

I'd Go to the Well With Him/ Her: *You can trust that person. One of LBJ's favorite forms of flattery.*

One Brick Shy of a Load: *Someone who's not too bright.*

Onery as a Tromped-on Rattlesnake: *About as mean as you can get.*

Parisfrance: *One word, as in, "We're goin' to Parisfrance," so folks won't think you're going to the Paris in northeast Texas.*

Plumb Tarred and Tuckered Out: *Exhausted, as in "That game was such a barn burner it left me plumb tarred and tuckered out."*

That Dog Won't Hunt: *Anything totally lacking merit, just as a hound dog that won't hunt is considered worthless.*

Who Put Jalapeños in His Grits? *Reaction to an action on the part of someone for whom "fixin' to" is usually a state of limbo. "Who put a burr under his saddle?" carries the same connotation.*

Yawl: *A contraction of "you all" never used in the singular, a point of Texan grammar outsiders fail to comprehend. One Texan may say to another, "Yawl come over real soon," or ask, "Yawl fixin' to go to the game?" The plural pronoun embraces the subject's entire family, right down to Aunt Minnie May and Cousin Jim Bob, even though they're not present.*

And then there's the weather. Mother Nature dotes on making television meteorologists look foolish. Old-timers' joints and bones make more accurate predictions than scientific data:

Blew the Fences From the Red River to the Rio Grande: *Description of a rip snortin' blue norther.*

Blue Norther: *Frigid air identified by a blue cloud on the north horizon rapidly moving south. Television meteorologists call it an Arctic cold front.*

Good Lord Willin' and the Creeks Don't Rise: *We'll be there come hell or high water.*

Norther: *Cold air.*

Rainin' Pitchforks and Horny Toads: *A drought breaker.*

FAVORITE BUMPER STICKERS

Texas: Love It or Leave It
Native Texan
Don't Mess With Texas
Secede
Lone Star and Long Necks: Only in Texas

I WASN'T BORN IN TEXAS, BUT I GOT HERE AS FAST AS I COULD

AUSTIN PROUD

DORSETT
MILE 221
221
TRUCK STOP
35

NATIVE TEXAN

TEXAS IMAGINEERING, SAN ANTONIO, TX

BEVO FOR PRESIDENT

Don't Mess With TEXAS

Personalities

Stories about the state's colorful personalities, native and adopted, fill many books. In the field of politics alone the list ranges from tobacco-chewing John Nance (Cactus Jack) Garner, an earthy South Texan twice elected U.S. vice president, to eloquent Barbara Jordan, the Houston congresswoman whose wisdom and sonorous voice captivated viewers during the Watergate hearings.

Every Texan has personal favorites, and the following are a sampling of mine.

Sam Houston

Sam Houston was destined to be a Texian, and not just because he grew to be six feet, six inches tall. Born in Virginia, as a young boy he lived with Tennessee Cherokees, who called him Coloneh, the Raven. At nineteen he began teaching school, even though his formal education was meager. Later, using borrowed books, he studied for six months and qualified to practice law.

His heroics as a volunteer during the War of 1812 gained the admiration, life-long friendship, and political patronage of General Andrew Jackson. At thirty Houston was a U.S. congressman, and at thirty-four he became governor of Tennessee. During his second term he married the eighteen-year-old daughter of a powerful Tennessee family. Less than three months later, his bride left him, for reasons Houston refused to discuss and no historian has managed to uncover.

The scandal almost drove Houston to suicide. Instead, he resigned the governorship and rejoined the Cherokee in the Oklahoma Indian Territory. This time they called him Ootsetee Ardeetahskee, the Big Drunk. He took an Indian wife, but left her behind when he decided to push on to Texas, where he quickly got caught up in the revolutionary cause.

As the hero of San Jacinto, he had no trouble twice being elected president of the republic. Between terms he courted and married a twenty-one-year-old Alabama belle. His unpopular concern for Indian rights and antislavery views as the state's first U.S. senator caused voters to refuse Houston's bid for the governorship in 1857. Two years later he won, but the victory turned hollow with Secession. Houston refused to take the oath of allegiance to the Confederacy. He packed up his wife and eight children and returned to their East Texas home in Huntsville, where he died at the age of seventy.

OPPOSITE PAGE: *Sam Houston, the Virginian who became a Texas legend.*

Elisabet Ney

Elisabet Ney was a century ahead of the times when she and her physician husband emigrated to Texas in 1875. As a student in her native Germany, the gifted sculptress applied for admission to the Munich Academy of Fine Art and went on a hunger strike until the board dropped a ban against females and admitted her. Ludwig II, Bavaria's "Mad King," was her patron and confidant. She considered marriage a "form of slavery," and retained her maiden name. That eccentricity, coupled with her penchant for wearing bloomerlike pants generated plenty of gossip in Texas during the nineteenth century. Her marble statues of Stephen F. Austin and Sam Houston grace the Capitol, and reproductions are in the Smithsonian.

Chester Nimitz

Japanese historians consider Lord Horatio Nelson, their own Heihachirō Togō, and Chester H. Nimitz the greatest naval strategists of all time; but most Americans know little about the man who became commander-in-chief of the Pacific Fleet during World War II. However, the native Texan's memory is revered in his Hill Country hometown, Fredericksburg, and in Japan.

Nimitz ranked seventh in the 1905 Naval Academy graduating class and rose to Chief of Naval Operations (1945 to 1946), despite an early career court-martial for grounding a destroyer in Manila Bay. He was a modest man who insisted that a postwar museum planned in his honor be dedicated to all military personnel who served in the Pacific theater. The Fredericksburg Museum is part of the restored Nimitz Hotel his grandfather built in the nineteenth century. Exhibits spotlight the admiral's family, life, and accomplishments as well as the Pacific campaign from Pearl Harbor through the Tokyo Bay surrender signing.

When word of the museum reached Japan in 1963, public subscription raised 250,000 dollars for a Garden of Peace. The Japanese government sent landscape experts, plantings, and craftsmen to Texas. They spent months in Fredericksburg designing an exquisite little Japanese garden around a replica of Admiral Togō's study, where Nimitz and his close friend spent hours discussing naval strategy before the Russo-Japanese War hero's death in 1934. The setting is a moving tribute to the fleet admiral who masterminded the destruction of Japan's naval power yet gained the respect of the country's people through his compassion during the postwar years.

OPPOSITE PAGE: *Fleet Admiral Chester Nimitz.* **BELOW:** *Admiral Nimitz signing the Japanese surrender treaty aboard the* U.S.S. Missouri *in Tokyo Bay.*

Ima Hogg

Contrary to a tale Texas schoolchildren still enjoy telling, Ima Hogg never had a sister named Ura. Her siblings were Will, Tom, and Mike, and her parents named their only daughter after the heroine in a poem written by her uncle, apparently with little thought to its connotation.

Her father, James Stephen Hogg, was Texas' first native-born governor, and after her mother's death, Ima assumed the role of family hostess at age thirteen. Although she never married, some of the world's most eligible bachelors are said to have courted the proud Houston beauty.

Several years after the West Columbia oil strike on the Hogg plantation, Varner, increased the family fortune, she and her brothers, Will and Mike, commissioned John Staub to design Bayou Bend. The home is still the showplace of River Oaks, the affluent Houston residential area the Hogg siblings developed. Ima filled Bayou Bend with priceless American antiques and early Texas furnishings; and when she was seventy-five, gave the entire estate to the Houston Museum of Fine Art.

"Miss Ima," as she was known throughout the world, restored Varner, furnished it completely with antiques, and gave it to the state. In a similar spirit of generosity, she gave Winedale, a collection of early nineteenth century structures in Central Texas, to the University of Texas when she was eighty-five years old.

Miss Ima was winding up an antiquing foray through Europe in 1975 when she slipped getting out of a London taxi and broke her hip. She died the next day at the age of ninety-three. To Texans the only connotation Miss Ima's name suggests is philanthropist.

William Sydney Porter

The American writer William Sydney Porter —better known to us today as O. Henry— came to Austin in 1882 and worked as a draftsman in the Old Land Office Building, which he used as the setting for the short story "Bexar Scrip No. 2692." Several years later, the author quit his job as a bank teller to devote his talents to editing the *Rolling Stone*, a satiric newspaper that was a literary, but not financial, success. He coined the term "violet crown" to describe the hillsides rimming the capital city, and the phrase became part of the local lexicon. Two years after leaving the bank he was charged with embezzlement, and eventually served time in a federal prison, where he continued to write under the pen name O. Henry.

RIGHT: *Ima Hogg was a wealthy Houston philanthropist and daughter of popular Texas governor James Stephen Hogg.* **OPPOSITE PAGE**: *While imprisoned for embezzlement, William Sydney Porter (seen here in front row, left) began writing short stories under the pseudonym of O. Henry. After his release, he continued to write under that name. His collected works of fiction were published in 1917 in fourteen volumes, seven years after his death.*

Chapter Three

THE FOOD

Hospitality is as much a part of Texans' nature as saying "Howdy."

The open house tradition began in frontier days when settlers shared food with newcomers passing through and put them up for as long as they needed to stay.

After the turn of the century guests came for days, or even weeks. In a rural society, folks were bound to be at home, tending to the livestock and chores.

Drop-in company was a joy—not the faux pas Miss Manners abhors today—and there was no question that they'd stay for supper—the lighter, more relaxed, 6 P.M. meal that signaled completion of the day's chores. Noon was considered dinnertime.

My mother could turn out dozens of fluffy, steaming biscuits, platters of sausages, and scrambled eggs without missing a conversational beat. The finest compliment you can pay a hostess is, "You set a mighty fine table," and it doesn't have a thing to do with the napery, china, or silver. Cooks beam if a dish is deemed "larrupin'."

Informality continues to be the keynote, and despite the heat and humidity (which Texans consider something of a badge of courage), backyards are the most popular places to entertain. From Central Texas southward, grilling on the patio and around the pool is enjoyed year-round.

Mexican cooks exerted the first influences on Texas cuisine with chilies and masa, the slaked cornmeal harina used to make tortillas.

In the nineteenth century, Southern settlers introduced home cooking when they brought in their talent for preparing fried chicken, biscuits, and rich, sweet cobblers and pies. In a spirit of making do, they substituted cornmeal for scarce and expensive wheat flour, peaches for apples, and pecans for walnuts. The pioneers' staple dish, beans and corn bread, is protein-rich and nutritionally balanced, as are the Mexicans' tortillas and frijoles.

From the chuck wagons came sourdough biscuits and barbecue, perfected by "cookies," who were pivotal to the success of a cattle drive or roundup.

The brewing skills of the German settlers produced what would become Texans' beverage of choice, beer; and their descendants' meat markets in New Braunfels, Fredericksburg, and Elgin are now famous for their tasty wursts, just as the bakeries of Schulenburg are renowned for kolaches, the filled Czechoslovakian pastries that were introduced by immigrants from Moravia and Bohemia.

Cajuns who came across from Louisiana into Southeast Texas substituted rice for potatoes and added a new array of spices and herbs as well as gumbo and jambalaya.

Szechuan, Thai, and Vietnamese dishes that sound foreign and taste familiar are contributions of the latest adopted Texans, whose family operations are reminiscent of those first Tex-Mex restaurants that made eating out so much fun.

Tex-Mex

Tex-Mex, the state's own cuisine, evolved when north-of-the-border cooks adapted south-of-the-border ingredients to Lone Star palates with sassy, but not too sizzling, results. To visit Texas and not sample Tex-Mex would be tantamount to passing up pasta in Italy. The culinary experience can create more memories than the Alamo, unless you overindulge in margaritas, the smooth tequila cocktails capable of causing legendary hangovers.

If you order chili in Mexico, you'll get a blank stare from the waiter—or you might be given a plate of jalapeños. The dish is Texan. Every amateur chef in the state thinks he or she makes the world's greatest chili, so an endless array of local chili cookoffs qualify competitors for the November championships at Terlingua, the Big Bend ghost town.

PAGE 69: Green chile and corn chowder. LEFT: Texans are born knowing the difference between chili and chilies, and outsiders think we're also endowed with flame-proof palates. Chili is the basis of Tex-Mex cuisine. BELOW: Chilies are a crucial ingredient in chili. Pictured here are various types of chilies.

© Steven Mark Needham/Envision

The traditional "bowl of red" is made by simmering meat, chilies, and the cook's personal blend of seasonings, which always includes cumin, a savory spice the first European settlers brought with them when they emigrated from the Canary Islands to San Antonio in 1731.

Purists grind their own spices, while the less ambitious rely on Two Alarm Chili Mix, a formula concocted by the late Wick Fowler, one of the first grand champions of the Terlingua World Chili Cookoff. The mix produces chili with canned heat ratings

© Amy Reichman/Envision

ABOVE: *A tall glass of cool iced tea is the perfect drink for a Tex-Mex meal.* **OPPOSITE PAGE:** *Fajitas are the latest addition to Tex-Mex menus.*

ranging from false alarm to two alarm. Autumn sparks a seasonal yearning, seemingly intuitive to Texans' taste buds, that only a bowl of chili can satisfy.

Like so many Lone Star legends, fact and fiction about the origin of chili have become more colorful through the years. Some say an innovative cook at the San Antonio jail cooked meat of questionable vintage with chilies and other spices to disguise the taste. The stew became so popular with inmates that they refused to leave after serving their sentences.

West Texans insist the first chili was devised by chuck-wagon cooks who made tough beef palatable through long, slow simmering and potent seasoning that satisfied the palates of cowboys accustomed to snacking along the trail on pequins, the small, fire-hot wild chilies.

It is true that during the nineteenth century San Antonio lavanderas (laundresses) cooked chili in their iron wash pots and sold the pungent stew around the city's plazas. The "chili queens" were joined by "tamale men," who peddled homemade tamales from pushcarts. The era ended in 1937 when modern health ordinances closed the state's original fast-food operations.

Instead of going out of business, the chili queens and tamale men moved indoors and opened restaurants in their barrio homes. Grandmother ruled the kitchen, mama and papa supervised the dining room, and children waited on tables. As business increased, additional rooms were furnished with secondhand tables and chairs. It was the food, and not ambience, that was important.

Menus were based on the regular plate: an enchilada, rice, refried beans, a tamale with chili gravy, and choice of a crisp taco or *chile con queso*, with either a pecan (puh-KAHN) praline, or lime or pineapple sherbet for dessert.

Substitution requests produced an array of combination plates, and by the late 1950s enterprising restaurateurs, like Matt Martinez of Austin's El Rancho, began putting the Tex-Mex touch on *chile rellenos*, *mole*, and *carne asada*.

Austin became so renowned for its excellent restaurants that Houston and Dallas establishments still advertise, "We serve Austin-style Tex-Mex."

Beer, served in an ice-cold mug, puts out the chilies' fire and complements each dish. Texans are loyal to Lone Star, Pearl, and Shiner brews. Next best is iced tea (ahst tea), preferably with lemon and without sugar.

The Fajita

Fajita, the thin skirt steak from cattle's ribs, was the ranch hands' reward for butchering. Chili-spiked marinades and quick charcoal grilling converted the less-than-choice cut into a delicacy. Given Texans' passion for barbecuing, it was only a matter of time before the fajita turned up on backyard grills. Thin slices of the beef, garnished with lettuce, chopped tomato, guacamole, grated cheese, and salsa, are rolled into a flour tortilla. The fajita's popularity increased its market value and led to such misnomers as chicken and shrimp "fajitas."

TEX-MEX
~ GLOSSARY ~

Like the cuisine, Tex-Mex pronunciation is distinctively different:

CHALUPA (Sha-LOOP-ah): *Flat fried tortillas covered with refried beans, melted cheese, chopped lettuce, and tomato.*

CHILE CON QUESO (Chilly kon-KAY-so): *Translates to chilies with cheese, but it's actually cheese with chilies: A Tex-Mex fondue served over tostadas or crisply fried flat tortillas.*

CHILI (Chill-ee): *The official state dish and mainstay of Tex-Mex cooking. A combination of coarsely ground or chopped meat, chilies, and spices is slowly cooked to the consistency of stew. Perfectly seasoned chili puts a glow, not blisters, on your palate. It is also called chili con carne or "bowl of red" and is usually served with crisp saltines crumbled into the chili. Dipping crackers into chili is considered mugrosa, or "unacceptable," and to purists the addition of tomatoes or beans during cooking is an unpardonable sin because it masks the perfect blending of spices.*

ENCHILADA (N-cha-LAH-duh): *A Tex-Mex crepe made by rolling grated cheese, chopped onion, and chili gravy into a soft corn tortilla. The enchilada is then topped with additional cheese, chili gravy, and onion and heated to bubbling. It's always served with the waiter's warning: "Hot plate, very hot plate."*

FRIJOLES (Free-HOLE-ays): *Boiled pinto beans mashed to a lumpy paste and reheated in hot lard. They are also known as refried beans, probably because the protein-rich leftovers were reheated for several meals.*

Corn tortillas, quartered and deep fried, are the preferred chip for Tex-Mex dipping. Shown here with a bean and chile pepper dip, they satisfy hungry appetites until the main course arrives.

GUACAMOLE (Wah-ka-MOLE-ay): *Avocado mashed with onion, lemon or lime juice, garlic, and the cook's secret ingredients. Texans add generous dashes of salsa. Used as a dip and a garnish for tacos, nachos, and salads.*

JALAPEÑO (Hal-uh-PAIN-yuh): *The most prevalent chile. It loses some of its fire when the seeds and veins, which contain capsaicin, are removed.*

MARGARITA (Mar-ga-REE-tah): *A cocktail of two parts tequila, one part Triple Sec or Cointreau, and one part fresh lime juice served in a salt-rimmed glass. The substitution of lime-flavored powder produces a ghastly green drink disdained as "Tex-Mex Koolaid." Variations include frozen margaritas, which some consider to be overpriced tequila-flavored snow cones.*

PICANTE (Pea-KAHN-Tay): *The standard Tex-Mex condiment of chopped chilies, tomatoes, garlic, cilantro, and onion with an impact ranging from tame to tear-jerking, depending on the amount you add. Jars are labeled mild, medium, and caliente (hot). For the uninitiated, even mild can be sinus-clearing.*

PRALINE (PRAY-lean): *Not even a close cousin to the European confection of the same name, the praline consists of a creamy, sugary base with pecans, dropped by the spoonful to harden into patties. Restaurants that add coconut for filler probably also serve ghastly green margaritas and use processed cheese spreads for nachos.*

SALSA: *Is to picante what fresh vegetables are to canned. Picante is processed and bottled, but salsa cruda is best about three hours after it's made. Pico de gallo, which translates to "rooster's beak," contains the same ingredients plus diced avocado, and is more relish than sauce.*

TACO (TAH-ko): *A folded, crisply fried tortilla filled with seasoned ground meat, shredded lettuce, chopped tomato, and grated longhorn cheese. Try to eat it with a fork and the shell will shatter all over the table and your dinner partners. Tacos are hand-held and eaten leaning over the plate so the juices don't dribble down your arm.*

TAMALE (Tuh-mal-E): *A Mexican hot dog of meat-filled masa (a lime-slaked corn flour) dough wrapped and steamed in dried corn shucks. Gerald Ford once showed his ignorance of Tex-Mex by attempting to eat a tamale without removing the husk— needless to say, he didn't win Texas in that presidential election.*

TORTILLA (Tor-TEA-yah): *A thin pancake made of masa. When buttered, spread with salsa, and rolled, tortillas are a bread. It is also the base for tostadas, nachos, enchiladas, tacos, and chalupas. Flour tortillas are a refined version unrelated to Tex-Mex.*

TOSTADAS (Tos-TAH-dahs): *Most people are familiar with these quartered, deep-fried tortillas that are dipped in salsa and nibbled while studying the menu and sipping margaritas. Top a tostada with refried beans, melted Monterey Jack cheese, and a jalapeño slice and it becomes a nacho, the ultimate Tex-Mex canapé.*

OPPOSITE PAGE: *Tacos are a Tex-Mex staple that have become a national favorite.*

Tolbert's Bowl of Red

Frank X. Tolbert, one of the founders of the International Chili Cookoff in 1967, was a purist who swore by this "scratch" chili recipe. Ancho chile pods are dried chile poblano.

6	TO 9 ANCHO CHILE PODS
3	POUNDS LEAN BEEF, COARSELY GROUND OR CHOPPED
1	TABLESPOON GROUND CUMIN SEED
1	TABLESPOON GROUND OREGANO
1	TABLESPOON SALT
½	TO 1 TABLESPOON GROUND CAYENNE PEPPER
1	TABLESPOON TABASCO
3	CLOVES GARLIC, MINCED
3	TABLESPOONS MASA HARINA

Wear rubber gloves to wash and remove stems and seeds from the dried chilies. Boil until skins slip off, about 30 minutes. Chop or grind, saving water to add to meat. (Eventually Talbot mellowed and allowed that 6 to 9 tablespoons of chili powder could substitute for the chilies.)

Sear meat in a small amount of fat until it turns gray. Add peppers and enough reserved water to cover. Simmer for half an hour. Add all ingredients except masa and simmer for an hour, covered, adding more water as needed. Stir in masa and cook 30 minutes.
SERVES 8.

OPPOSITE PAGE: *Not all salsas are created equal, but all are made with fresh ingredients. These spicy salsa dips were made with fresh chopped vegetables, spices, and herbs. Cilantro is a favorite herb for Tex-Mex dishes, giving them a distinct flavor.* **BELOW:** *Some of the ingredients commonly used in Tex-Mex cuisine.*

Saucy Salsa

The quality of the salsa can make or break a Tex-Mex restaurant. It must be fresh and piquant. Salsa is best prepared about an hour before serving so ingredients can blend. It should be used the day it's made.

Serrano chilies are the small, tapered green chilies about an inch and a half long. The oils are volatile and irritating to the eyes, so wear gloves when chopping and wash hands well when the job is completed.

1	MEDIUM TOMATO, CHOPPED
5	SPRIGS CILANTRO, CHOPPED
2	OR 3 SERRANO CHILIES, CHOPPED
3	SCALLIONS, CHOPPED
½	CLOVE GARLIC, CRUSHED

Add the chopped tomato, cilantro, chilies, and scallions, including the green part, to the crushed garlic. Add salt.
MAKES ½ CUP.

Guacamole

Guacamole should be lumpy—not a smooth paste.

2	AVOCADOS, PEELED
1	TABLESPOON GRATED ONION
1	TABLESPOON LEMON OR LIME JUICE
½	CLOVE GARLIC, CRUSHED
1	PEELED TOMATO, FINELY CHOPPED
	SALT AND SALSA (TO TASTE)

Mash the avocado, but don't puree. Add onion, citrus juice, and garlic, and blend. Fold in chopped tomatoes, salt, and salsa a teaspoon at a time.
MAKES 1½ CUPS.

Texas Barbecue

Texas provided the necessary ingredients—beef and hardwood—and Mexico contributed the word, *barbacoa*, which became known as barbecue.

Remember that scene in *Giant* in which Elizabeth Taylor faints at the sight of the pièce de resistance served during the barbecue given in her honor? It wasn't apocryphal. Whole steer cooked over pits of red-hot coals that were part of every trail drive still are de rigueur at ranch fiestas and rodeos, and the prolific pesky mesquite that demands constant clearing remains the ideal slow-burning hardwood.

The barbecue tradition spread to towns, where farmers and ranchers came in on Saturday in order to buy supplies. Most families were large and cash was usually short, so eating in the local café or fancy restaurant was out of the question. Enterprising butchers dug pits in back of their markets and smoked any meat that wouldn't keep until Monday. Barbecue was sold by the pound and was eaten from the paper wrapping along with bread and pickles that were brought from home.

You still find some of Texas' best barbecue in small towns. Authentic, down-home barbecue stands have wood stacks in back and squeaky screen doors. "Cash Only" and "No Shirt, No Shoes, No Service" signs and the high school football schedule, preferably with a squad picture, decorate smoke-blackened walls. Don't be surprised if the knives are chained to the scarred Formica-topped tables.

Briskets must cook for seven to eight hours, so the cook starts working long before dawn. By 2 P.M. he's ready to call it a day, and he'll close the place earlier if demand exceeds supply.

Sliced or chopped brisket, sausage (called "hot guts"), ribs, and chicken are the usual options. Pork is an East Texas mainstay, and in the Rio Grande Valley, *cabrito*, young goat, is popular.

Orders are served with plain, spongy white bread, sour pickles, onion slices, and peppery sauce. Potato salad, cole slaw, and pinto beans are optional. Few places have liquor licenses, so instead of Lone Star in long-neck bottles, the house beverage is iced tea.

Old-time professionals disdain the thick, sweetened sauces backyard amateurs

OPPOSITE PAGE: *A summer picnic: iced tea, fried chicken, biscuit, and pecan pie.*

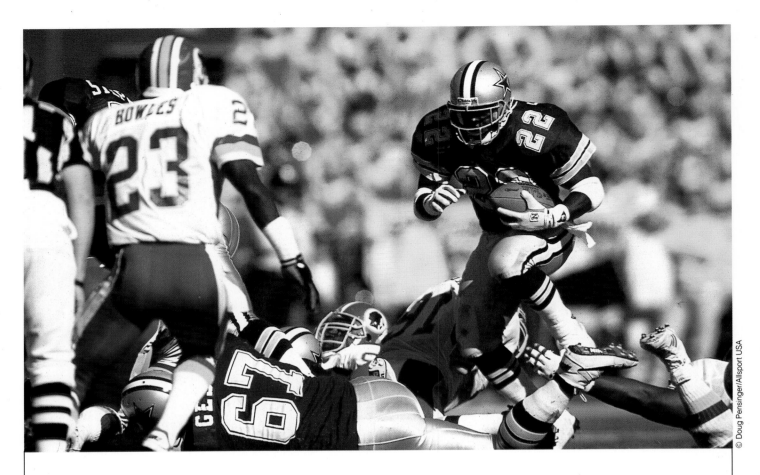

© Doug Pensinger/Allsport USA

concoct, primarily because sugar sparks flare-ups that burn the meat. Some only use a mixture of vinegar and oil for "soppin'" after rubbing the meat with salt and pepper, because they believe smoke alone produces the finest flavor. Others season tomato juice with Tabasco, Worcestershire sauce, and vinegar for a thin basting that stimulates smoke by dripping on the hardwood coals.

Texas barbecuers all swear by the smoking method but differ on the wood. Mesquite is the most popular, although post oak has its fans, too. Some throw mesquite beans and pods on the coals, while others think wet pecan shells produce a superior flavor.

Weekend vendors are a common sight along busy highways, where they cook and sell from "Texas hibachis," fifty-gallon drums converted to smokers.

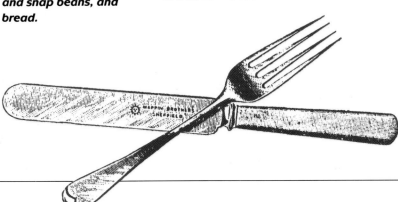

Food and Football

Outsiders believe that Texans consider football more a religion than a sport, and they may be right. Friday nights are devoted to high school teams, usually nick-named Bears, Tigers, Wildcats, or Eagles, although the Taylor Ducks, Hutto Hippos, Itasca Wampus Cats, Munday Moguls, and Port Lavaca Sandcrabs are colorful exceptions. It would be heresy to schedule any other event on Friday night from early September until mid-November, when losers fold their tents and winners move into the playoffs, which finally decide the state champions on the weekend before Christmas.

On Saturday, the fans switch their faith to universities and colleges. Pregame and halftime extravaganzas combine show business with sports as bands, pom-pon squads, twirlers, and cheerleaders go all out. At Longhorn games in U.T. Austin's Memorial Stadium, 300 student handlers roll out a Lone Star flag that covers the playing field and triggers a rendition of "Texas Fight," accompanied by the roar of the burnt-orange-clad fans and a sea of "hook 'em horns," the trademark hand signal.

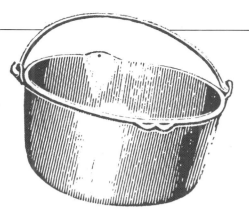

Sunday is set aside for the Cowboys and the Oilers.

Parking lots swarm with tailgate parties that begin hours before the stadium gates open and pick up where they left off after the game. A group of my Houston friends bought an air-conditioned motor home to guarantee ideal tailgating conditions, and no one thought it a bit unusual.

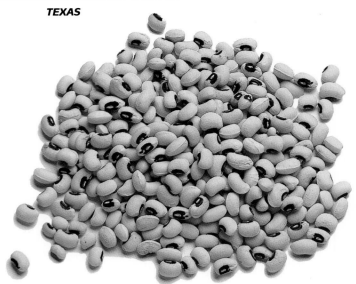

Cook the peas, ham bone, vegetables, garlic, and seasonings in water for 2 to 3 hours, or until peas are soft. Add water as liquid boils down.

Remove bone and allow peas to cool slightly before blending the mixture smooth in a food processor fitted with the metal blade. Return to soup pot, stir in beef bouillon and sliced sausage. Cook for half an hour. Stir in sour cream, and reheat. Season with salt and pepper.
SERVES 10 to 12.

Grapefruit and Avocado Salad

Helen Corbitt came to Austin from New York in 1940 to teach institutional cooking at the University of Texas and manage the University Tea Room. Years later she recalled being appalled at Texans' preference for fried and overcooked foods. She blazed culinary paths at the Driskill Hotel in Austin, the Houston Country Club, and the Neiman-Marcus Zodiac Room, where Stanley Marcus described her as "the Balenciaga of food." One of her tastiest combinations was Rio Grande Valley grapefruit segments and avocado slices garnished with poppy seed dressing.

Salad

3	MEDIUM-SIZE RUBY RED GRAPEFRUIT
3	AVOCADOS
	POPPY SEED DRESSING (SEE BELOW)
	GREENS FOR GARNISH

Peel the grapefruit, divide into segments, and remove membrane before cutting into bite-size pieces. Peel and dice the avocados. Toss grapefruit and avocados with dressing. Serve in a salad bowl lined with lettuce leaves.

If serving on salad plates, leave the grapefruit segments intact. Halve the avocados lengthwise and divide into 12 slices. Alternate grapefruit and avocado slices, using 3 of each for individual servings.
SERVES 12.

Cotton Bowl Watching Buffet

Television football coverage sparks game-watching parties, particularly on New Year's Day, when the Southwest Conference champion is the Cotton Bowl's host team. Here is a menu of Texas favorites.

Black-Eyed Pea Soup
Grapefruit and Avocado Salad
Corny Jalapeño Cornbread
King Ranch Chicken
Peggy's Pralines

Black-Eyed Pea Soup

Black-eyed peas in some form are mandatory, since eating them on the first day of the year generates good luck.

3	CUPS DRIED BLACK-EYED PEAS
	BONE FROM THE CHRISTMAS HAM
2	CUPS EACH DICED CELERY, ONION, AND CARROTS
2	GARLIC CLOVES
2	TABLESPOONS CHILI POWDER
3	QUARTS WATER
3	CUPS BEEF BOUILLON
2	SMOKED SAUSAGE LINKS, THINLY SLICED
1	CUP SOUR CREAM
	SALT AND PEPPER (TO TASTE)

© Steven Mark Needham/Envision

Tangy avocado and grapefruit salad served with blue cheese instead of poppy seed dressing is an appealing variation on a Texas tradition.

Poppy Seed Dressing

1½	CUPS GRANULATED SUGAR
2	TEASPOONS DRY MUSTARD
1½	TEASPOONS SALT
⅔	CUP WHITE VINEGAR
3	TABLESPOONS FINELY GRATED ONION
2	CUPS SALAD OIL (NOT OLIVE OIL)
3	TABLESPOONS POPPY SEEDS

Mix sugar, dry mustard, salt, and vinegar in a blender or food processor fitted with the metal blade. Blend in onion; add oil slowly, blending constantly, and continue blending until thick. Blend in poppy seeds.

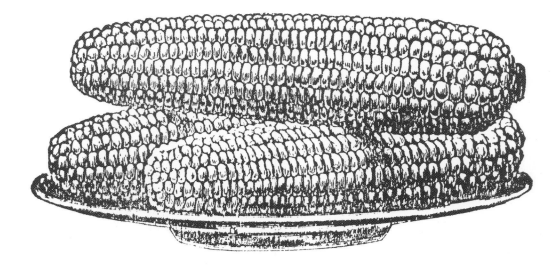

Corny Jalapeño Cornbread

Texans don't add sugar or flour to cornbread, and prefer yellow cornmeal over white. Put a heavy iron skillet, muffin or corn-stick pans greased with bacon drippings in the oven to heat while you're mixing the batter.

2	CUPS YELLOW STONE-GROUND CORNMEAL
1½	TEASPOONS SALT
3	TEASPOONS BAKING POWDER
1	TEASPOON BAKING SODA
1	CUP FROZEN WHOLE KERNEL CORN, THAWED
4	TABLESPOONS CHOPPED PICKLED JALAPEÑO (SEE NOTE)
3	TABLESPOONS GRATED ONION
1	CUP GRATED MONTEREY JACK CHEESE
2	CUPS BUTTERMILK
2	EGGS, LIGHTLY BEATEN
2	TABLESPOONS BACON DRIPPINGS

Preheat oven to 400 degrees F.

Sift the dry ingredients together in a bowl. Add the corn, jalapeño, onion, and cheese and mix well, coating the corn and other ingredients. Combine the buttermilk, eggs, and bacon drippings. Fold liquid into the dry ingredients and blend well, but don't beat. Pour batter into a 10-inch, hot, greased iron skillet and bake 30 to 35 minutes in preheated oven. Alternatively, use 18 hot, greased corn-stick or muffin pans and bake in preheated oven for 15 to 20 minutes.

NOTE: For milder flavor, use 2 tablespoons canned green chilies, chopped, and 2 tablespoons pickled jalapeño. For tender palates, use all green chilies.
SERVES 6 TO 8.

King Ranch Chicken

No Lone Star cookbook is complete without some version of this casserole, which may or may not have originated on the world-famous South Texas spread.

2	THREE- TO FOUR-POUND FRYERS
1	LARGE ONION, QUARTERED
2	CLOVES GARLIC
2	TEASPOONS SALT
8	SPRIGS CILANTRO
1	10-OUNCE CAN ROTEL TOMATOES (SEE NOTE)
12	CUPS WATER

Bring all the ingredients to a boil in a large kettle. Skim fat off the top, cover, and simmer 2 hours. Remove chickens from pot, peel off skin, and debone. Set meat aside.

Return skin and bones to kettle and simmer another hour, adding water as necessary to cover ingredients and produce 6 cups of broth. Strain through a fine sieve.

NOTE: Rotel is the brand name for canned tomatoes with chilies. If unavailable, substitute a cup of mild picante.

Sauce

1	STICK BUTTER OR MARGARINE
¾	CUP ALL-PURPOSE FLOUR
6	CUPS CHICKEN BROTH
2	CUPS HALF-AND-HALF
¾	CUP PICANTE (OR TO TASTE)
1	8-OUNCE CAN CHOPPED GREEN CHILIES (*NOT* JALAPEÑOS)

Melt butter or margarine, and stir in flour to make a smooth roux. Combine broth and half-and-half and add slowly to the flour mixture, stirring until thickened and smooth. Stir in picante and green chilies. If the dish is to be frozen or refrigerated for later use, allow sauce to cool before continuing. Then prepare the following:

24	CORN TORTILLAS, CUT INTO 1-INCH-WIDE STRIPS
9	CUPS BITE-SIZE CHICKEN PIECES
1	POUND MONTEREY JACK CHEESE, GRATED
1	POUND SHARP CHEDDAR CHEESE, GRATED
1	CUP CHOPPED ONION
3	2-QUART CASSEROLES, BUTTERED

Preheat oven to 325 degrees F.

Each casserole requires strips of 8 tortillas. Starting with a layer of tortilla strips, add Sauce, 1 cup of chicken, and a generous sprinkling of combined cheeses and onion. Repeat 2 times and top with additional cheese. Warm in preheated oven for 45 minutes to an hour, or until cheese melts and sauce bubbles.

SERVES 18.

© Lois Ellen Frank

Freshly harvested green chilies are the secret ingredient to many a Tex-Mex dish.

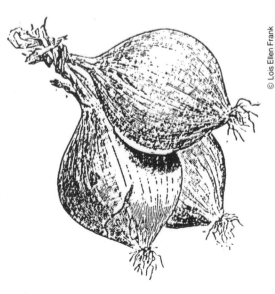

Peggy's Pralines

The name of the person who gave you a recipe automatically becomes part of the title, so the files of Texas cooks are filled with treats like these.

2   CUPS GRANULATED SUGAR
¾   TEASPOON BAKING SODA
1   CUP HALF-AND-HALF
1½   TABLESPOONS BUTTER OR MARGARINE
2   CUPS PECAN HALVES AND QUARTERS

Cook sugar, baking soda, and half-and-half over medium heat until mixture reaches soft ball stage or 234 degrees F on a candy thermometer. Stir constantly to avoid scorching. Remove from heat and add exactly measured butter or margarine. Beat until mixture begins to stiffen and turn creamy, then stir in pecans. Drop on waxed paper by the teaspoonful, and allow to cool and harden.

Pecans are the crucial ingredient in Peggy's Pralines.

Texas Originals

In 1976, an Austin newspaper columnist, Larry Besaw, wrote a tongue-in-cheek story about the origins of chicken-fried steak. He attributed the culinary coup to a mythical café, Ethel's Homecooking, in Lamesa. Other columnists and publications picked up Besaw's fiction and have printed it as fact so often that aficionados go to the West Texas town searching in vain for the home of chicken-fried steak. The origin of the Lone Star favorite, like that of pickled okra, can't be traced. Both evolved from the need to adapt available ingredients to Texans' tastes.

Chicken-Fried Steak

Interlopers have been known to describe chicken-fried steak and cream gravy as sole of shoe with over-peppered Elmer's glue, but who cares? We dote on the dish, which has become a mainstay of down-home cooking. According to a Texas Restaurant Association estimate, 800,000 orders of chicken-fried steak are served throughout the state *every day.*

1	BONELESS ROUND STEAK, CUT ½-INCH THICK
2	EGGS
¼	CUP MILK
	SALT AND PEPPER (TO TASTE)
1	CUP ALL-PURPOSE FLOUR
	COOKING OIL

Flatten the meat with a tenderizing mallet and cut into serving-size pieces. Beat the eggs with the milk and add seasonings to the flour. Dip the steak in the liquid, then dust well with flour. Repeat. Shake off excess flour. Heat about an inch of cooking oil in a heavy skillet. Fry the steak to a golden brown, turning halfway through the cooking. Drain on paper towels. Transfer to a warm platter while you make the gravy.

Cream Gravy

4	TABLESPOONS DRIPPINGS
4	TABLESPOONS ALL-PURPOSE FLOUR
2	CUPS MILK
	SALT AND PEPPER (TO TASTE)

Let the browned batter particles settle in the skillet before draining off all but 4 tablespoons of the cooking oil. Stir in the flour and cook over low heat until roux is barely golden. Gradually add milk and cook until gravy thickens. Season to taste. Pour over steak.

Pickled Okra

Some Texans prefer pickled okra to popcorn as a snack food. You'll need 6 pint jars with lids for this recipe.

3	POUNDS TENDER YOUNG OKRA PODS
6	SMALL RED CHILIES
6	CLOVES GARLIC
6	LARGE DILL HEADS WITH STEMS OR 3 TEASPOONS DILL SEED
1	QUART WATER
1	PINT WHITE VINEGAR
½	CUP SALT

Divide washed, whole okra pods into 6 portions and pack into 6 heated pint jars with chile, garlic clove, and dill. Make a brine of the water, vinegar, and salt; heat to boiling, and pour over okra. Seal jars and process 20 minutes in boiling water (timing begins when the water reaches the boiling point).
MAKES 6 PINTS.

Okra came to Texas tables by way of the deep South, where it was usually boiled or combined with chicken to make a gumbo.

～ FRITO FACTS ～

The Frito, like Dr. Pepper, is a Texas original that wasn't sold outside the state for many years. Frito pie is a menu mainstay at concession stands where the three-ounce sack is split on the side, the Fritos are doused with half a cup of chili gravy, topped with grated longhorn cheese and chopped onion, and micro-waved until the cheese melts.

Frito pie also is a standard at small-town Dairy Queens, along with chili dogs, corny dogs (hot dogs dipped in cornbread batter and deep-fried), and steak fin-gers, a variation of chicken-fried steak. The red-roofed "D.Q." is the nerve and social center of more than 800 small Texas towns. The prefabricated franchise serves as a gossip command post on the community's busiest highway intersection, where comings and goings are duly monitored by customers and employees who know everyone in town and most of those in the surrounding coun-tryside. Retirees meet there for coffee, teenagers hang out at the D.Q., and fans gather in the booths to second-guess the coach after the Friday-night game. If you're looking for someone or seeking information, the Dairy Queen is the first place to stop. The entrance of a stranger is sure to halt conversation.

Wine Country

In the 1880s, Texas rootstock helped rescue the European wine industry when the *Phylloxera* scourge threatened to wipe out the vineyards of France, Germany, and Italy. Dr. T.V. Munson of Denison shipped roots of louse-resistant North Texas varieties to Europe, where viticulturists successfully grafted the hardy vines to white riesling, chardonnay, pinot noir, and cabernet sauvignon vinifera and saved the industry.

RIGHT: *Susan and Ed Auler of Fall Creek Vineyards toast their award-winning vintages. The Aulers ferment their wines in French oak barrels, puncheons, and stainless steel tanks.* OPPOSITE PAGE: *Although California is typically considered the wine-making center of the United States, Texas has approximately twenty-five wineries of its own.*

© Courtesy of Texas Highways Magazine

After Prohibition only one winery remained in Texas. Val Verde in Del Rio survived by using the vineyard's grapes for jellies and jams. Texans' natural preference for beer, iced tea, or "bourbon and branch" made the state a meager market for wine until 1971, when new liquor laws ended brown-bagging and allowed restaurants to have bars, a profit-making sideline.

The advent of the 747 sent enterprising young people jetting to Europe, where they discovered the delights of foreign cuisines. Many came home and opened trendy cafés featuring dishes only wine could complement, which spurred a revival of wine making throughout the state. At last count, there were twenty-five wineries producing a wide variety of vintages, and one, Moyer in New Braunfels, that makes nothing but champagne.

Fall Creek Vineyards

Wine became a new focus in the lives of Susan and Ed Auler almost twenty years ago, when the couple went to France in order to buy cattle for their Hill Country ranch. While touring Burgundy, they were struck by the great similarity between the soil, terrain, and climate of the Côte d'Or and their Fall Creek Ranch.

The vineyards that the Aulers began as an experiment now produce prize-winning wines, particularly the Fall Creek Vineyards Emerald Riesling, which has been hailed by experts as the finest bottling of that white wine.

The excellent wines bring gourmets, international sommeliers, premier chefs,

and a host of other interesting people to Fall Creek Vineyards' striking setting on Lake Buchanan. Dean Fearing of the Mansion on Turtle Creek and Stephan Pyles of Route Street Café and Baby Routh, two of the country's innovative young chefs, developed special dishes designed to match Fall Creek wines served in their Dallas restaurants.

Susan says Texas-style entertaining means "at home" to her. The occasion, be it a hunting house party or a harvest celebration, sparks a theme, guest list, entertainment, and good food and wine.

Susan's menus feature what she calls "our wonderful Texas bounty." Hill Country peaches, beef and lamb, fresh cheese from the Mozzarella Company in Dallas, native peppers and herbs, Texas pecans, seafood, and fish are among her favorite ingredients.

Bouquets of beautiful wildflowers in straw baskets, dried arrangements of native grasses and pods, and fragrant pots of herbs offer decorating opportunities that succeed in accentuating the atmosphere of warm, friendly informality.

"Entertainment oftentimes is country-and-western recording artist Loy Blanton, and the food is always Texan," Susan says.

Texas Bounty Patio Grill For Six

This is one of Susan's favorite menus.

Shrimp Quesadillas with Red Pepper Sauce
Grape Leaves Stuffed with Hill Country Lamb
Grilled Catfish and Black Bean Chimichangas with Avocado Mayonnaise
Mixed Fresh Garden Greens
Peach Bread Pudding with Lemon Sauce

OPPOSITE PAGE: *Quesadillas can be fancy, such as Shrimp Quesadillas with Red Pepper Sauce, or simple, like these with melted cheese and guacamole on the side.*

Shrimp Quesadillas with Red Pepper Sauce

Serve appetizers with Fall Creek Vineyards Sauvignon Blanc.

6	TABLESPOONS (APPROXIMATELY) UNSALTED BUTTER
2	CLOVES GARLIC, FINELY MINCED
2	TABLESPOONS FINELY MINCED SHALLOT
1	POUND MEDIUM-SIZE SHRIMP, PEELED AND DEVEINED
1	TABLESPOON LEMON JUICE
3	TEASPOONS FINELY MINCED PICKLED JALAPEÑO SLICES
3	TABLESPOONS FINELY MINCED CILANTRO
3	CUPS GRATED MONTEREY JACK CHEESE
	SALT AND FRESHLY GROUND PEPPER (TO TASTE)
12	6-INCH FLOUR TORTILLAS

Melt 4 tablespoons butter in a heavy skillet. Sauté the garlic and shallot until translucent but not browned. Add shrimp and lemon juice and sauté about 5 minutes, or until the shrimp are pink and slightly curled. Remove from heat.

Mince the shrimp and place in a mixing bowl with garlic/shallot mixture, japaleño, and cooking juices. Add fresh cilantro and cheese; season with salt and pepper.

Mix well and divide into 12 equal portions. Melt 1 tablespoon of remaining butter in an 8-inch, nonstick skillet. One by one, soften the tortillas by quickly heating one side in the hot butter. Add additional butter to the skillet as necessary. Mound shrimp mixture on half the buttered side of the warm tortilla. Fold over to form a half circle and press edges to seal. Cut each half into 3 wedges with a very sharp knife. Place on a plate, garnish with fresh cilantro leaves, and serve with Red Pepper Sauce. **MAKES 36 QUESADILLAS.**

Red Pepper Sauce

3	TABLESPOONS MINCED SCALLION
1	TABLESPOON MINCED GARLIC
2	TABLESPOONS UNSALTED BUTTER
1½	CUPS RED PEPPER, ROASTED, PEELED, AND SEEDED
1	CUP CHICKEN STOCK
1	TABLESPOON LEMON JUICE
1	TABLESPOON SALT

Sauté scallion and garlic in butter. Blend red pepper, chicken stock, lemon juice, and salt in a food processor fitted with the metal blade until smooth. Add this to the onion/garlic mixture in the skillet and heat until well blended. Serve hot with quesadillas.

Grape Leaves Stuffed with Hill Country Lamb

You may wish to accompany this recipe with a dip or sauce of plain yogurt seasoned to taste with lemon juice and coarse salt.

24	(1 JAR) MEDIUM-SIZE PRESERVED GRAPE LEAVES
½	POUND VERY LEAN LAMB, GROUND
1	CUP CANNED ITALIAN PLUM TOMATOES, CRUSHED
½	CUP UNCOOKED TEXAS LONG-GRAIN RICE
½	CUP EXTRA-VIRGIN OLIVE OIL
1	BUNCH SCALLIONS, CHOPPED
1½	CUPS LOOSELY PACKED FRESH MINT LEAVES, CHOPPED
	JUICE OF 1 LEMON

Drain and separate the grape leaves. Rinse carefully under running water and set aside. Combine lamb, tomatoes with liquid, rice, olive oil, scallions, and mint.

Lay a grape leaf, vein side up, stem toward you, on the work surface. Place 1 tablespoon of the filling at the base of the leaf and roll up, tucking in the sides to form a small bundle. Repeat with remaining filling and leaves, packing each bundle, seam side down, in a small kettle. Squeeze lemon juice over the bundles and add water to almost cover. Weight with a heat-proof plate.

Cover, bring to a boil, then reduce heat and simmer for 1 hour, or until rice in stuffing is completely cooked. Serve hot, or refrigerate in the cooking liquid to serve cold.

MAKES 24 STUFFED GRAPE LEAVES.

Grilled Catfish and Black Bean Chimichangas with Avocado Mayonnaise

This recipe accents the buttery almond succulence of farm-raised catfish. This dish is best when served with Fall Creek Vineyards Chardonnay.

1	TABLESPOON MINCED GARLIC
2	TEASPOONS MINCED BASIL *OR* CILANTRO
1	CUP SAFFLOWER OIL
6	CATFISH FILLETS
	SALT AND PEPPER TO TASTE

Combine the garlic, basil or cilantro, and oil. Pour over fillets and marinate for 1 hour. Remove fillets and set the remaining marinade aside to make the Avocado Mayonnaise later. Grill the fillets over charcoal or any aromatic wood for 4 to 5 minutes on each side, being careful not to overcook. Season with salt and pepper. Keep warm.

Black Bean Chimichangas

4	CUPS COOKED BLACK BEANS
2	TABLESPOONS FINELY CHOPPED GARLIC CHIVES
3	TABLESPOONS FINELY CHOPPED CILANTRO
½	TEASPOON SALT
½	TEASPOON FRESHLY GROUND PEPPER
1½	TABLESPOONS POBLANO PEPPER, MINCED
18	FLOUR TORTILLAS
8	TO 10 OUNCES TEXAS GOAT CHEESE
	PEANUT OIL FOR FRYING

Combine beans, herbs, and seasonings in a food processor fitted with the metal blade and blend, leaving beans lumpy. Steam tortillas to soften. Place 1 tablespoon bean mixture and 1 teaspoon goat cheese in the center of each tortilla. Fold sides in and cover with top and bottom flaps. Secure with toothpicks. Heat oil in a heavy skillet and deep-fry chimichangas until golden. Remove toothpicks before serving.

MAKES 18 CHIMICHANGAS.

Avocado Mayonnaise

1	TABLESPOON BALSAMIC VINEGAR
1	RIPE AVOCADO
½	TEASPOON SALT
1	TABLESPOON LIME JUICE
1	TEASPOON DIJON MUSTARD
3	EGG YOLKS
	REMAINING MARINADE

Strain the garlic and basil or cilantro from the fillet marinade. Combine these seasonings with the vinegar and reduce in a small saucepan. Puree avocado, salt, and lime juice in a food processor fitted with the metal blade or a blender. Add reduced basil and garlic, mustard, and egg yolks. Blend until smooth, then add remaining marinade and blend until creamy. Serve warm over grilled fillets and chimichangas.

OPPOSITE PAGE: *Grape Leaves Stuffed with Hill Country Lamb—a perfect dish to serve at an informal backyard party.*

Mixed Fresh Garden Greens

1	HEAD OAK-LEAF LETTUCE
16	SORREL LEAVES
1	SMALL HEAD RADICCHIO
4	CARROTS

Arrange greens in an attractive composition on 8 individual salad plates. Cut carrots in an Oriental slicer to form a spiral. Position half of each carrot curl on each salad.

Dressing

1	CUP EXTRA-VIRGIN OLIVE OIL
⅓	CUP RASPBERRY VINEGAR
1	TABLESPOON BROWN SUGAR
¼	TEASPOON ANCHOVY PASTE
2	TEASPOONS MINCED FRESH BASIL *OR* TARRAGON

Blend ingredients well and dress greens.
SERVES 8.

Peach Bread Pudding with Lemon Sauce

Stonewall peaches give a Texas twist to Susan Auler's bread pudding recipe. A 1987 Fall Creek Vineyards Johannisberg Riesling complements this dessert.

2	CUPS HALF-AND-HALF OR LIGHT CREAM
½	CUP MILK
½	CUP SOUR CREAM
2	TEASPOONS LEMON JUICE
5	EGGS, BEATEN
¾	CUP GRANULATED SUGAR
¼	CUP BROWN SUGAR
⅛	TEASPOON SALT
2	CUPS FRENCH BREAD, THINLY SLICED AND TORN INTO PIECES
½	CUP TOASTED PECANS, CHOPPED
2	CUPS SLICED FRESH PEACHES

Preheat oven to 350 degrees F.

In the top of a double boiler whisk cream, milk, sour cream, and lemon juice. Heat just to boiling. Beat eggs with ½ cup of the granulated sugar, brown sugar, and salt. When liquid is very hot, whisk in the eggs a little at a time and cook until slightly thickened. Butter a soufflé dish and arrange bread pieces evenly on the bottom. Top with toasted pecans. Arrange peaches over pecans and sprinkle with remaining ¼ cup of sugar. Pour in lemon cream and bake in a hot water bath in preheated oven for 1 hour.

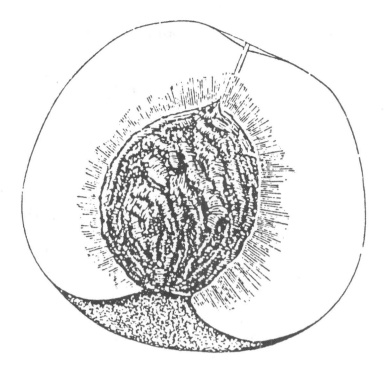

Lemon Sauce

1	CUP GRANULATED SUGAR
¼	TEASPOON SALT
½	PINT HEAVY CREAM
4	TABLESPOONS UNSALTED BUTTER
4	TEASPOONS GRATED LEMON RIND
8	TABLESPOONS FRESH LEMON JUICE

Stir sugar and salt together. Add cream and cook over low heat until thick, stirring constantly. Remove from heat, stir in butter, lemon rind, and lemon juice. Serve over hot bread pudding, garnished with lemon slices and fresh mint.
SERVES 6 TO 8.

Pride House Hospitality

Anyone who disdains breakfast hasn't feasted on that meal at Pride House. When Ruthmary Jordan opened one of Texas' first bed-and-breakfasts in historic Jefferson, her friends thought she'd taken leave of her senses, and there must be times when the vivacious hostess agrees! She turned a gingerbread Victorian house into a model of Lone Star hospitality, where guests become family as soon as they step foot across the threshold.

OPPOSITE PAGE: *Instead of lemon sauce, try an orange marmalade with your bread pudding.*

Ruthmary says she'd almost rather scrub floors than write down a recipe, not because she doesn't want to share her kitchen's bounty but because she cooks from experience and an innate sense of how good food tastes, not from prepared instructions.

The Pride House breakfast menu changes daily. Guests serve themselves at leisure in the main hallway. During the summer, bright zinnias in stoneware pitchers decorate the polished buffet. Glowing copper containers with autumn-hued chrysanthemums are fall favorites, and happy red and hot pink geraniums in terracotta pots brighten winter mornings. Fine china, crystal, and silver give the breakfast trays elegant touches.

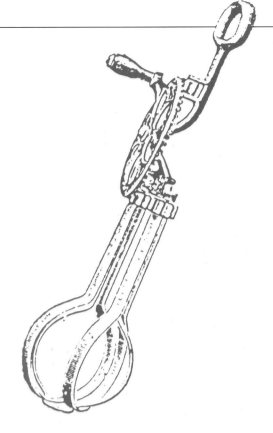

Bran Spice Muffins

OPPOSITE PAGE: *Bran muffins are a treat no matter what the time of day.*

Due to constant requests, Ruthmary finally agreed to write down and test recipes for her guests' favorite muffins.

The combination of spices in these muffins fills Pride House with a mouthwatering aroma that makes waking up a special pleasure.

6	TABLESPOONS SHORTENING
⅓	CUP GRANULATED SUGAR
2	EGGS
1⅓	CUPS ALL-PURPOSE FLOUR
2	TEASPOONS BAKING POWDER
¼	TEASPOON EACH ALLSPICE, CLOVES, MACE, AND SALT
1¼	CUPS MILK
3	CUPS BRAN FLAKES

Preheat oven to 375 degrees F.

Cream shortening and sugar. Add eggs and continue creaming. Sift dry ingredients together—except for bran flakes—and add to creamed mixture alternately with milk, ending with flour, and stirring only to blend. Lightly fold in bran flakes. Bake in greased muffin tins 5 minutes in preheated oven. Reduce temperature to 350 degrees F and bake 10 minutes longer.

MAKES 24 MEDIUM-SIZE MUFFINS.

Lemon Almond Muffins

Ruthmary gets up long before dawn to do her baking, but Lemon Almond Muffins can be frozen and heated in the microwave.

1	CUP SHORTENING
1	CUP GRANULATED SUGAR
4	EGG YOLKS, WELL BEATEN
2	CUPS ALL-PURPOSE FLOUR
2	TEASPOONS BAKING POWDER
½	TEASPOON SALT
½	CUP LEMON JUICE
4	EGG WHITES, STIFFLY BEATEN
2	TEASPOONS GRATED LEMON PEEL
1	TEASPOON ALMOND EXTRACT

Preheat oven to 375 degrees F.

Cream shortening and sugar, add egg yolks, and beat well. Alternately add sifted dry ingredients with lemon juice. Mix lightly but don't beat. Fold in egg whites, lemon peel, and almond extract. Bake in greased muffin tins in preheated oven for 15 to 20 minutes.

MAKES 1½ DOZEN MEDIUM-SIZE MUFFINS.

Chapter Four

GARDENING

Late March through April, depending on nature's whim, is the period when the Texas landscape casts winter's dull coat aside and erupts with color. No matter what the calendar says, the first bluebonnet sighting means spring is here. Of course, Texans also keep a wary eye on the mesquite, because the native trees are far more reliable at forecasting a late freeze than meteorologists. It's a folk-tale fact that mesquite won't leaf out until the danger of frost is past.

Like most everything else in Texas, gardening and landscaping have no set pattern. Palms that flourish in the Rio Grande Valley wouldn't live through a single Panhandle winter. East Texas is as boggy as West Texas is dry.

Botanists divide the state into ten distinct regions with more than 500 soil types and a wide range of climates that produce a marvelous contrast of native plant life, trees, shrubs, and wildflowers.

Nature is a factor no amount of scientific study can predict or generalize. The intense, four-day freeze in December 1989, which sent temperatures plummeting to record-breaking single digits as far south as San Antonio and the low teens in the Rio Grande Valley, destroyed the Ruby Red grapefruit industry. Growers and scientists are presently testing and searching for a comparable variety that will be able to survive through such freakish periods of intense bitter cold.

Obviously there's nothing anyone can do to control Texas' weather, but we can scrutinize it and learn from the past. Historian T.R. Fehrenbach makes the point that successful farmers and ranchers weren't the ones who prayed for rain, but rather those who studied Texas weather cycles and adapted.

Drought is one of the state's most dreaded conditions. Researchers who analyzed a century of weather patterns predict that the 1990s will be a drought-plagued decade. The forecast is stimulating interest and experiments in xeriscape, the landscaping concept with a name derived from the Greek word for "dry," *xeros*. Native plants, once scorned by gardeners as weeds, are showing up in custom-designed outdoor settings, which are nothing like the cactus plantings many people erroneously equate with xeriscape. Sure, cacti have a decorative spot in such plans, but water conservation gardens can be lush and green, too.

Texans began getting serious about native plants in 1982, when Lady Bird Johnson founded the National Wildflower Research Center outside Austin. The former first lady is a conservation champion whose enthusiasm provides momentum for beautification projects everywhere. But there's no question that her heart's at home in Texas, particularly in the spring when her Hill Country ranch is knee-deep in wildflowers.

Xeriscape

Simply put, xeriscape is the gardening art of working with nature instead of against it.

Experts outline seven steps for achieving water-efficient landscapes, which is the plan's—and gardener's—goal:

Planning and design: Consider the space usage and exposures, remembering that southern and western exposures have higher water requirements because they receive more sun during the moisture-depleting seasons. Don't plant grasses in narrow strips or corners that make maintenance difficult.

Limiting turf areas: Grasses' matted roots require more water than any other planting, but if your usage plan includes a recreational area, turf may be necessary. Select a native grass. One of the most popular and highly recommended for the Southwest, Midwest, and High Plains is buffalo grass (*Buchloë dactyloides*). Another grass with low moisture requirements is blue grama (*Bouteloua gracilis*).

Irrigating efficiently: Thorough, infrequent soaking mimics nature's best rains and nurtures deep roots, since soil stores the water. Sprinklers are fine for turf areas that need more moisture than plantings, and drip systems are ideal for ground covers, trees, and shrubs.

Improving soil: This involves advance planning, preferably three months before planting, so the compost, sand, or other additives necessary to give the soil the texture of loam can settle. A gravel or sand base is best for areas where you plan to plant wildflowers that don't like "wet feet."

Mulching: Three to four inches of mulch will reduce weed invasion, evaporation, and heat damage. The best mulch is coarse, such as bark chips.

Selecting plants: Go native, with plants that have low water demands. Plant shrubs for peace and privacy and trees for shade, to cool your house, and conserve energy. Don't put a plant with high water demands next to one that prefers arid conditions.

Maintenance: Until your xeriscape plan is established, it must be nurtured. It won't take the time and effort traditional landscaping requires, but don't think you can sit on the porch and watch your yard flourish. Clipping, pruning—and, yes, weeding—keep plants and shrubs shaped up and encroachments out.

PAGE 103: *Purple Coneflower* (Echinacea purpurea). **OPPOSITE PAGE:** *Maximilian Sunflower* (Helianthus maximiliani). *From July through October this tall, leafy perennial brightens Texas roadsides with an abundance of large golden flowers.*

Wildflowers and Their Cultivation

In Texas it isn't April showers that bring May flowers. Hot, dry summers, followed by cold, wet winters produce spring's best wildflower shows throughout the Lone Star State.

The harsh summers and winters curtail the competitive winter grasses—rye grass, purple vetch, fescues, and clover—that are wildflowers' worst enemies, because the species choke out tender young plants. Since Bermuda, bluestem, and St. Augustine go dormant in the winter, wildflowers can coexist with those grasses. Eradication is the only solution when introduced winter grasses take over wildflower sites.

Instead of turning an entire yard over to wildflowers, experts suggest combining color with native grasses, such as buffalo, Indian, little bluestem, and sideoats grama, for a managed xeriscape look.

Areas that are difficult to maintain, like corners and slopes, are ideal locations, since wildflowers reduce mowing and cut watering maintenance.

Border a vegetable garden with plantings, and the blooms will attract honey bees and butterflies.

You don't need a large cultivation space to enjoy growing wildflowers, either. Wooden barrels and all sizes of clay pots can create pleasing patio displays. Plant small pots to use as gifts.

Once you've selected a site, rake the area to loosen the soil surface to a depth of about one-half inch.

Bluebonnets are particularly vulnerable to competition from winter grasses because the low-growing plants must have sun, which the tall winter grasses block out. The state flower doesn't like having "wet feet" either, and grows best on slopes.

Site selection is vital to successful cultivation. General guidelines include choosing locations with little or no competing grasses, minimum foot traffic, a water supply, and at least six hours' sunlight daily, because if you don't have sun, you won't have blooms, and without blooms, there can be no reseeding.

If you're planting a mix, blend the seed in a bucket, because small seeds tend to filter to the bottom. To increase volume and aid distribution, combine the seed with a carrier, such as sand, top, or potting soil, at a ratio of four parts material to one part seed.

After hand-broadcasting the mixture, lightly rake the area to establish seed and soil contact. If it doesn't rain, keep the soil moist until germination, which will be completed by January. Varieties that go dormant following seedling establishment need water in early spring.

OPPOSITE PAGE: *Blue Grama* (Bouteloua gracilis). *This short, native perennial grass is most nutritious.* **LEFT:** *Sideoats Grama* (Bouteloua curtipendula). *The state grass of Texas.*

Botanists at Wildseed Incorporated, the largest company in the country engaged in harvesting and selling wildflower seeds, recommend moderate fertilization only when the soil lacks nutrients. A slow-release fertilizer of one part nitrogen, three parts phosphorus, and two parts potassium (8-24-16) is best.

Don't fertilize established plants, because you'll get lots of foliage and few flowers, which in turn limits reseeding.

The native annuals (plants that complete their life cycle in one year) and perennials (plants that return season after season) will return in increasing numbers years after year if allowed to reseed. For about two weeks after the full blooming period, when the seeds are maturing, the plants will look quite scruffy, but let them go to seed. Then mow the area down to four to six inches, and let nature take over.

No matter which part of the United States you live in, Wildseed has a flower mix to suit your climate and soil. Seven wildflower mixes are available, as well as a shade mix recommended for all parts of the country.

OPPOSITE PAGE: *Texas Bluebonnet* (Lupinus texensis). *This, the state flower of Texas, is found throughout the state in early spring blanketing fields and roadsides with its deep blue color and filling the air with a sweet fragrance.* **INSET:** *Mexican Hat* (Ratibida columnaris). *The Mexican hat is one of Texas' most common wildflowers. This easily recognizable member of the sunflower family can be found nodding along most Texas roadways from March through November.*

FAMILIAR TEXAS ～WILDFLOWERS～

It would be impossible to even list all the native plants that fall into the category of "wildflowers." The description fits at least 1,000 of the more than 5,000 flowering plant species known to grow naturally in Texas. This is a sampling of some of the most familiar wildflowers that lend themselves to cultivation from available commercial seed.

Indian Blanket (*Gaillardia pulchella*)
Deep orange to red yellow-tipped petals surround brown centers on this sprightly flower. The drought-tolerant perennial thrives in the Texas heat and intense sun. It makes an excellent cut flower that lasts a week or more in bouquets.

Lemon-Mint (*Monarda citriodora*)
This flower sounds like it should be yellow, but lemon-mint ranges from soft mauve to deep purple. The name comes from the citrus aroma the leaves release when crushed. Whorls drifting down the plant's single square stem attract hummingbirds and butterflies and make a brisk flavored tea when dried.

Mexican Hat (*Ratibida columnaris*)
The Mexican hat has a wilted look created by drooping, yellow-tipped red flowers surrounding a dark brown to black cone-shaped head; however, it makes an excellent cut flower and will last up to ten days in bouquets.

Moss Verbena (*Verbena tenuisecta*)
This hardy lavendar perennial is seen in fields throughout most of the state as soon as the danger of freeze ends. Butterflies hover over the flower clusters, which look like miniature nosegays. Moss verbena is a prolific reseeder.

Pink Evening Primrose (*Oenothera speciosa*)
The flower and its sister, the yellow evening primrose, are "buttercups" to Texans. Dusting the yellow pollen on your nose is a rite of spring that makes children of all ages giggle and most sneeze. The pale pink blossoms are a pleasing background for the bright bluebonnets.

Texas Bluebonnet (*Luninus texensis*)
All bluebonnets have been designated as the official state flower, but this is the most common variety. Lupines in the Big Bend grow almost two feet tall. The bluebonnet enriches the soil and other plant life with nitrogen when it completes its life cycle and decays.

Texas Paintbrush (*Castilleja indivisa*)
Actually an herb that takes its bright red color from bracts on a single stem that cradle the plant's tiny, creamy white flower, the Texas paintbrush is an early bloomer along highways throughout the state.

Tickseed (*Coreopsis lanceolata*)
This drought-tolerant perennial blooms from May through July. Although it normally takes two years to begin flowering, the foliage makes an attractive ground cover. The tickseed lends itself well to cutting, too.

Decorating With Wildflowers

While wildflowers are beautiful in their outdoor habitats, many lend themselves to cut flower bouquets, too. A basket brimming with bright blossoms is a delightful decoration. Many varieties can be used cut or dried so you can enjoy wildflowers all year.

Black-eyed Susan (*Rudbeckia hirta*), coneflower (*Rudbeckia amplexicaulis*), lemon-mint (*Monarda citriodora*), Mexican hat (*Ratibida columnaris*), purple coneflower (*Echinacea purpurea*), and yarrow (*Achillea millefolium*) are the varieties wildflower experts recommend both for cutting and drying.

The lacy white bishop's weed (*Ammi majus*) doesn't do well in fresh bouquets, but it dries nicely if you tie stems together and hang the blossoms upside down for several weeks until all moisture is removed.

Indian blanket (*Gaillardia pulchella*), butterfly weed (*Asclepias tuberosa*), cornflower (*Centaurea cyanus*), dense blazing-star (*Liatris spicata*), Drummond phlox (*Phlox drummondii*), gayfeather (*Liatris pycnostachya*), mealy sage (*Salvia farinacea*), moss verbena (*Verbena tenuisecta*), oxeye daisy (*Chrysanthemum leucanthemum*), plains coreopsis (*Coreopsis tinctoria*), scarlet sage (*Salvia coccinea*), standing cypress (*Ipomopsis rubra*), tahoka daisy (*Machaeranthera tanacetifolia*), Texas bluebell (*Eustoma grandiflorum*), and tickseed (*Coreopsis lanceolata*), are native species recommended for delightful bouquets, along with the domesticated rocket larkspur (*Delphinium ajacis*).

Where to See the Displays

When weather conditions comply, the Highland Lakes and Hill Country around Austin are the best areas to enjoy wildflower displays, which usually peak the first two weeks in April. The National Wildflower Research Center provides updates on conditions, beginning in mid-March.

All is not lost if nature doesn't cooperate. Wildseed Incorporated, the largest company in the country engaged in harvesting, selling, and commercially planting wildflower seeds, cultivates about a thousand acres in the Eagle Lake area.

The spectacle of dense, three-foot-wide row plantings of wildflowers stretching across the lovely rural countryside west of Houston invites comparison with Holland's world famous tulip fields. Tours usually begin the last week of March and continue through April.

OPPOSITE PAGE: *Texas bluebonnets and Texas paintbrushes (also known as Indian paintbrushes) color a field near Chapell Hill, the site of an annual bluebonnet festival.* **FOLLOWING PAGE:** *Yellow Evening Primrose (Oenothera spp.). Also known as the Texas buttercup, this clear yellow spring flower opens near sunset and closes the next morning.*

Spring in East Texas

East Texas puts on its own spring floral show. The Piney Woods are dense with dogwood and redbud, two flowering native trees that burst into bloom for about three weeks. The dogwood's delicate, shimmery white flowers and the deep wine of the redbud are a dramatic contrast to the woods' dark green pines.

About the same time, azaleas bloom in Houston, Tyler, and Dallas. The azaleas aren't native, but with expensive pampering they do well in certain areas. Showy displays in the gardens of Bayou Bend at Houston and along Dallas' Turtle Creek stop traffic.

~ TYLER ROSES ~

If you have a rose garden, odds are strong the bushes came from Tyler, an East Texas city that produces more than half the field-grown rose bushes sold in the country each year. Blooms peak from mid-May through October, when the annual Tyler Rose Festival celebrates the city's best-known crop.

© David Langford

Dogwood (Cornus florida). The white blooms of this small tree are some of the first signs of spring in East Texas.

Trees

Shade is a precious commodity in Texas. It takes some of the sting out of hot summer weather, and promotes energy conservation by protecting homes from the sun.

According to the Checklist of United States Trees, 222 varieties of trees are native to the land of Texas. Of that number I've selected a sampling that thrive in all or most of the state.

Cottonwood (*Populus deltoides*)

The male of this species is cottonless, a lack many Texans prefer. The tree, in one variety or another, grows throughout the state. In West Texas you can spot a homesite on the horizon by the cottonwoods rising out of the plains. The stands take on a golden glow in autumn that belies the cottonwood's reputation as a trash tree.

Crape Myrtle (*Lagerstroemia indica*)

The crape myrtle isn't native, but it's called the "Texas lilac," and we probably should adopt it as our own. It can be a tree, a bush, or a low shrub now that miniature and dwarf hybrids are available. The crape myrtle seems to flourish on benign neglect and loves full sun, something we have plenty of during July and August, when the plants produce full heads of tiny blossoms in white, pink, lavender, and watermelon-red, the most popular shade.

Live Oak (*Quercus* spp.)

Live oak trees can make you yearn to be a poet. Gnarled limbs sprawling out from the evergreens' thick trunks create gigantic canopies across the landscape and stand sentinel above graves in country church cemeteries. The variety is the perfect decoration for the Hill Country's limestone terrain, because live oaks keep their leaves throughout the winter and quickly trade the old for a new set in the spring. *A Field Guide to Texas Trees* identifies forty-three species of two varieties indigenous to the state, but I think the live oaks (*Quercus virginiana*) have the most character.

OPPOSITE PAGE: *Spanish Oak (Quercus falcata). This tree is a fall favorite with its orange- or bronze-colored autumn leaves. In spring, it displays bright Granny Smith-green leaves.*

Mesquite (*Prosopis fuliflore*)

This classic leguminous tree or shrub covers (some say infests) more than sixty million acres of rangeland. There shouldn't be a shortage of grilling wood for generations to come, because the mesquite resists eradication and drops seeds that can remain dormant for decades. The delicate, lacy leaves are no indication of the tree's strength and tenacity. Craftsmen form the hard wood into beautiful bowls, livestock thrive on the seedpods, and bees produce a particularly fine honey from the sweet-smelling flowers—all that and great barbecue, too. Maybe the mesquite should be the state tree.

Mountain Laurel (*Kalmia latifolia*)

The mountain laurel is as hardy as its name. Glossy, dark-green leaves and a profusion of deep purple flowers blooming in fragrant clusters, coupled with the mountain laurel's tolerance for conditions of either full or partial sun, make the slow-growing, drought-tolerant ornamental tree ideal for xeriscape.

Pecan (*Carya illinoensis*)

Pecan orchards fill rural river bottoms. The stream may be dry, but you know it was there when you see stand after stand of stately pecans towering fifty feet above the ground. If there is one tree within squirrel-range in your neighborhood, you're sure to find pecan shoots in odd places where the bushy little rodents chose to hide the nuts. A member of the hickory family, the pecan can live three centuries. Perhaps because it supplies the nuts for pecan pies and pralines, two favorite treats, the pecan has been named the state tree.

Willow (*Salix* spp.)

Willows were the sight settlers prayed for as they made their way across the wilderness, because the trees meant water. Along river banks and around stock ponds the delicate willows prevent erosion and smart gardeners leave them there. Transplanting the short-lived species around a garden pond may seem aesthetic, but the willow's roots are notorious for getting tangled up with the plumbing.

Garden Plantings

These plantings savor the Texas climate.

Begonia (*Begonia* spp.)

Look fragile, grow hardy. Also can be moved indoors when the cold weather of winter approaches if they are planted in pots or hanging baskets.

Caladium (*Caladium* spp.)

Great favorites because the leafy tubers have a cool look and like shade.

Chrysanthemum (*Chrysanthemum* spp.)

Some regions get two bloomings from chrysanthemum plants, the first in early spring and the second in the autumn when the flowers are expected. Extensive plantings in Lubbock make the High Plains city a chrysanthemum center.

Coleus (*Coleus* spp.)

Also likes shade and does well in hanging baskets and patio pots as well as in beds. Cuttings are easy to root and coleus can come indoors for the winter to add color to a sunroom.

Daylily (*Hemerocallis* spp.)

Lovely in rock gardens and good for holding soil in bank plantings. New varieties are even more colorful and bloom for a longer period of time.

Geranium (*Geranium* spp.)

Super pot plants for color around pools and patios. Trailing ivy-leafed varieties do well in hanging baskets. Geraniums appreciate at least partial shade during July and August.

Impatiens (*Impatiens* spp.)

Great for shady locations, pots, and hanging baskets. The flowers decrease as the heat increases, but get new life and bloom until frost.

Kalanchoe (*Kalanchoe* spp.)

Once thought of only as an indoor plant, kalanchoe grows well outdoors, particularly the common red variety. Easily grown from rootings, it doesn't need rich soil or fertilizing, and with a bit of cover can survive freezing weather.

© Wanda La Rock/Envision

OPPOSITE PAGE: *The hardy zinnia, in all its many colors, has long been a favorite bedding plant in Texas.* **LEFT:** *Kalanchoe (Kalanchoe blossfeldiana). This colorful, easy-to-grow succulent from Madagascar is a favorite of Texas gardeners. It flourishes outdoors in full sun or semi-shade until late in the year, and if brought indoors with its blooms pinched back, it will flower again during the winter months.*

Marigold (*Tagetes* spp.)

A native of the Southwest and Mexico, so it adapts well to hot, dry summers. Some gardeners plant marigolds among tomatoes to ward off nematodes.

Rose (*Rosa* spp.)

From hybrid teas to antiques, roses are an all-time Texas favorite, and Tyler nurseries develop species for all parts of the state.

Zinnia (*Zinnia* spp.)

A mixture of miniature and standard zinnias creates interesting, colorful flower beds. The secret is to plant twice each season, first in early spring, after the danger of frost is past, and again the first week of July, so you'll have zinnias blooming through fall.

Cacti

Cacti seem a homely—even ugly—lot, until you see the usually colorless plants gussied up with fabulous, satiny blossoms that outshine any rainbow.

Many people mistakenly believe that the yucca, century plants, sotols, and agaves are members of the cactus clan. In fact, all of these plants are actually members of the lily family. The allthorn and ocotillo, which also prefer a desert habitat, aren't types of cacti, either.

The flat-padded prickly pear is the most familiar variety, and the easiest for cartoonists to sketch. It's also the most commonly used garden planting. *Cacti of Texas* lists ninety varieties within the *Opuntia* genus, prickly pears' botanical identification. If prickly pears were money, Texas could pay off the savings and loan debt.

NEAR RIGHT: *It's not the long spines on the prickly pear cactus that sometimes cause the inattentive hiker problems—they are easy to see and remove—it's the red, ¹/₄-inch ones at the base that once in your skin or clothing, seem impossible to locate and remove.* **FAR RIGHT:** *The small mariposa cactus grows in the Big Bend section of Texas, blooming from March to July. Its delicate white petals are a favorite food of rodents and numerous birds.*

© David Langford

In his 1947 book, *Adventures with a Texas Naturalist,* Roy Bedichek wrote, "Botanists assign fearsomely cumbrous names, sometimes two or three, each cluttered up with the name of an individual who fathered it, and they are all duly frozen in print for the great convenience of scientists scattered about over the world; but you can't use these names in flesh and blood conversations."

Cacti seem about as suited to Latin designations as they are to petting, so just call them prickly pears, cow-tongues, strawberry, button, fishhook, pin cushion, devil's head, night-blooming cereus, and all the other descriptively plain names people have been using to identify different species for generations.

Sources For Texas Products

For Foodstuffs:

Caliente Chili Inc.
Drawer 5340
Austin, TX 78763
Wick Fowler's Two Alarm Chili Mix, ranked
best by *Consumer Reports*.

Collin Street Bakery
401 West Seventh
Corsicana, TX 75110
Ships fruit cakes and Texas pecan cakes
all over the world.

County Line
1-800-344-RIBS
Barbecued ribs, brisket, and sausage air-
freighted to your door within forty-eight
hours.

Das Peach Haus
Rt. 3 Box 118
Fredericksburg, TX 78624
Ships Stonewall peaches in season and
jams and jellies all year.

El Galindo
1601 East Sixth
Austin, TX 78702
Crunchy tostadas by the bag or box.

Granada Foods
2901 Polk
Houston, TX 77003
Sunday House smoked turkeys, Texas
beef steaks, fajita-style marinated meats,
and flash-frozen, pond-raised shrimp.

Guadalupe Pit Smoked Meats
1299 Gruene Road
New Braunfels, TX 78130
Specializes in vacuum-packed barbecued
pork and beef, sausages, turkeys, ancho-
cilantro and other special cheeses. Catalog on request.

Jardine's Texas Foods
Box 18868
Austin, TX 78760
Features D.L. Jardine's Chili Works, the
mix that won the *Washington Post* critics'
award, and a variety of specialty products
in boxes. Free brochure on request.

La Grange Meat Market
Box 520
La Grange, TX 78945
Smoked turkeys, turkey sausage, bite-size
and link jalapeño dry sausage.

Lammes
Box 1885
Austin, TX 78767
Originated the Texas Chewie Pecan Pra-
line and its chocolate covered cousin, the
Texas Longhorn. Say "Lambs."

Mozzarella Company
2944 Elm Street
Dallas, TX 75226
Produces and ships its own version of the
Italian classic and a variety of other
cheeses.

New Canaan Farms
Box 386
Dripping Springs, TX 78620
The mother lode for jalapeño mustard,
shrimp sauce, catsup, and jelly, plus hon-
eys, fruit butters, and sugar-free spreads.

Pace Foods
Box 12636
San Antonio, TX 78212
Mild, medium, or hot Pace Picante by the
jar or by the gallon.

San Saba Pecan Inc.
2803 West Wallace
San Saba, TX 76877
Native and cultivated shelled pecans,
pecan brittle, and pralines.

Talk O' Texas Brands
1610 Roosevelt
San Angelo, TX 76905
Specializes in pickled okra.

Texas Duet
Box 26529
Austin, TX 78755
Texas wildflower honey, spicy Pecan Pick-
ins, Texas Praline Sundae Sauce, pecan
pies, and special gift baskets.

Texas Fruit Baskets
1126 Hollow Creek #2
Austin, TX 78704
Provides the ultimate Texas care package:
picante, Artesia mineral water, chili mix,
tostadas, Hill Country honey, and pecans,
or design your own.

Texas Traditions
Rt. 1 Box 123B
Georgetown, TX 78626
Mesquite Bean Jelly, Red Chili Pepper
Jelly, Prickly Pear Cactus Jelly, Jalapeño
Pepper Jelly, Texas Hot Salt, and gift
boxes.

Wilson Pecos River Bison Co.
Box 12940
Odessa, TX 79768
Ships lean, healthy buffalo steaks.

For Seeds and Plants:

Antique Rose Emporium
Rt. 5 Box 143
Brenham, TX 77837
Specializes in antique roses and Victorian
garden plantings. Send five dollars for
catalog.

Bob Wells Nursery
Box 606
Lindale, TX 75771
Ships roses, flowering shrubs, berry and
grape vines, fruit, nut, and shade trees.
Free catalog.

It's About Thyme
729 East FM 1622
Austin, TX 78748
Lists 206 plants and herbs grown free of
pesticides or chemicals, and also ships
seeds. Catalog on request.

Lily Ponds Water Gardens
Box 188
Brookshire, TX 77423
Features water lilies, daylilies, and other
plants.

Tate Roses
Rt. 20 Bx 436
Tyler, TX 75708
Hybrid teas, floribundas, and climbers are
among seventy-six varieties of patent and
standard Texas-grown roses. Free brochure on request. No California ship-
ments.

Wildseed Inc.
Box 308
Eagle Lake, TX 77434
For top-quality wildflower and native
grass seeds developed for all parts of the
country.

Other Sources:

National Wildflower Research Center
2600 FM 973N
Austin, TX 78725
Spring wildflower hotline, March 20 to
May 31, Texas only.

Pride House
4009 East Broadway
Jefferson, TX 57657

Gardens to Visit:

Bayou Bend Gardens
1 Westcott
Houston, Texas 77007-7009

Botanic Gardens
University Drive at IH-30
Fort Worth, Texas 76107

Corpus Christi Botanical Gardens
8500 South Staples
Corpus Christi, Texas 78413

Dallas Arboretum and Botanical Gardens
8525 Garland Road
Dallas, Texas 75218

Judge Roy Bean Visitor Center
Loop 25 off SH 90
Langtry, Texas 78871

Lajitas Desert Garden
Highway 170
Lajitas, Texas 79852

Mercer Arboretum and Botanic Gardens
22306 Aldine-Westfield Road
Humble, Texas 77338

Municipal Rose Garden
1800 West Front Street
Tyler, Texas 75710

San Antonio Botanical Gardens
555 Funston Place
San Antonio, Texas 78209

Zilker Park Garden Center
2220 Barton Springs Road
Austin, Texas 78746

For More Information

In the United States, call the Tourism Division of the Department of Commerce toll-free: (800) 888-8TEX, or write Texas, Box 5064, Austin 78763-5064. Among the free materials available are an official highway map, travel handbooks, a quarterly calendar of events, a list of campgrounds, and a guide to commonly seen wildflowers and shrubs.

The official state travel magazine, *Texas Highways,* published by the Travel and Information Division, Texas Highway Department, is an award-winning publication featuring stories and photographs about places of interest throughout the state. Subscriptions are $12.50 a year ($20 for foreign addresses). Write to Customer Service, Box 5016, Austin, TX 78763-5016.

Bibliography

Nonfiction

Bedichek, Roy. *Adventures with a Texas Naturalist.* Austin: University of Texas Press, 1984.

Brook, Stephen. *Honky-Tonk Gelato: Travels Through Texas.* New York: Atheneum, 1985.

De la Pena, Jose Enrique. *With Santa Anna in Texas.* Translated and edited by Carmen Perry. College Station: Texas A&M University Press, 1975.

Dobie, J. Frank. *A Vaquero of the Brush Country.* Austin: University of Texas Press, 1981.

———. *Cowpeople.* Austin: University of Texas Press, 1981.

———. *Tales of Old-Time Texas.* Austin: University of Texas Press, 1984.

———. *The Longhorns.* Austin: University of Texas Press, 1980.

———. *The Mustangs.* Austin: University of Texas Press, 1984.

Frantz, Joe B. *Texas.* New York: Norton Press, 1976.

Haley, James. *Texas: An Album of History.* New York: Doubleday, 1985.

Kutac, Edward A. *Birder's Guide to Texas.* Houston: Gulf Publishing Company, 1989.

Leckie, William. *The Buffalo Soldiers.* Norman: University of Oklahoma Press, 1986.

Newcombe, W.W. Jr. *The Indians of Texas.* Austin: University of Texas Press, 1961.

Phares, Ross. *Texas Traditions.* New Orleans: Pelican Books, reprinted 1975.

Steitz, Quentin. *Decorating With Texas Naturals.* Austin: University of Texas Press, 1987.

Wasowski, Sally. *Native Texas Plants, Landscaping by Region.* Austin: Texas Monthly Press, 1988.

Webb, Walter Prescott. *The Texas Rangers: A Century of Frontier Defense.* Austin: University of Texas Press, 1965.

Fiction

Bird, Sarah. *Alamo House.* New York/London: Norton, 1986.

Ferber, Edna. *Giant.* New York: Fawcett, reprinted 1979.

Kelton, Elmer. *The Wolf and the Buffalo.* College Station: Texas A&M University Press, 1986.

McMurtry, Larry. *Lonesome Dove.* Austin: S&S Press, 1985.

McMurtry, Larry. *The Last Picture Show.* New York: Penguin, 1979.

Thompson, Thomas. *Blood and Money.* New York: Doubleday, 1976.

To Guide You

The Roads of Texas, a 168-page, full-size atlas detailing every highway, road, city, town, community, and facility in the state can be obtained from Shearer Publishing, 406 Post Oak Road, Fredericksburg, TX 78642. The cost is $12.95 plus $2 shipping; call (800) 458-3808 for credit card orders.

Index

Abrazo Ceremony, 18
Adair, John, 32
Adventures with a Texas Naturalist
    (Bedichek), 120
Agriculture
    botanical diversity, 102
    drought and freezes affecting, 102
Alabama-Coushatta Indians, 26
Alamo, battle at, 49
Allen brothers, 23
Amarillo, 33
Apache Indians, 52
    horse-riding skills, 46
Aransas National Wildlife Refuge, 21
Aransas Pass, 21
Astrodome (Houston), 25
Auler, Ed, 92
Auler, Susan, 92-94
Austin, 35-36
Austin, Stephen F., 35, 49, 63
Autry, Gene, 54
Avocado Mayonnaise, 97

Balcones Escarpment, 35
Barbecues, 81-82
Bass, Sam, 56
Beaumont, 26
Bedichek, Roy, 120
Begonias, 119
Besaw, Larry, 90
Big Bend National Park, 12
Big Cypress Bayou, 27
Big Thicket National Preserve, 26
Black Bean Chimichangas, 97
Black-Eyed Pea Soup, 84
Blacks, as cavalry "Buffalo Soldiers," 52
Blanton, Loy, 94
Bluebonnet, 108
Blues, 54
Bonnie and Clyde, 56
Bran Spice Muffins, 100
Bread
    bran spice muffins, 100
    jalapeño cornbread, 86
    lemon almond muffins, 100
Brownsville, 17
Bryan, John Neely, 29
Buffalo Bayou, 23, 25
Buffalo Soldiers, 52
Bumperstickers, 60
Bush, George, 18, 40

Cacti, 120
Caddo Lake, 26
Caladium, 119
Capitol building, 37
Capitol Syndicate, 32
Caprock Escarpment, 32
Chalupa, 74
Cherokee Indians, 63
Chicken-Fried Steak, 90
Chile con queso, 74

Chili, 74
    recipe, 78
    as Texas dish, 71-72
Chisholm Trail, 18
Chrysanthemums, 119
Climate, 10
Coleus, 119
Colt, Samuel, 56
Comanche Indians, 32, 52
    horse-riding skills, 46
Compromise of 1850, 10
Congress Avenue Bridge (Austin), 36
Corbitt, Helen, 84
Cornbread, 86
Corny Jalapeño Cornbread, 86
Corpus Christi, 18
Cottonwood tree, 116
Country-Western music, 54-56
Cowboys, rodeos and, 57-59
Crape myrtle tree, 116
Cream gravy, for Chicken-Fried Steak, 90

Dallas, 29
Daylilies, 119
Declaration of Independence (Texas), 49
Dialect, 59-60
Dressings
    for mixed green salad, 99
    poppy seed, 85
Drought, 102

East Texas, 26
    springtime floral shows in, 114
Edwards Plateau, 35-36
El Paso, 13
Emancipation Proclamation, 51
Empresario system, 47
Enchiladas, 74
Europeans, early settlements by, 52
Evening primrose, 108

Fajitas, 72
Fall Creek Vineyards, 92-94
Fearing, Dean, 94
Flipper, Henry O., 52
Food
    barbecues, 81-82
    fajitas, 72
    football and, 82-83
    influences and variety, 68
    Tex-Mex, 71-72
    Tex-Mex glossary, 74-76
    See also specific foods and recipes
Football, food and, 82-83
Ford, John S., 17
Fort Worth, 30
Fowler, Wick, 71
Frijoles, 74
Fritos, 91
Fruit
    lemon sauce, 99
    peach bread pudding, 99

Galveston, 22
Garden greens, 99

Gardening
    botanical diversity, 102
    cacti, 120
    drought and freezes affecting, 102
    garden plantings, 119
    trees, 116
    wildflower cultivation, 107-8
    xeriscape, 105
Garner, John Nance, 63
Geraniums, 119
Golden Triangle, 26
Goodnight, Charles, 32
Gould, Jay, 27
Granger, Gordon, 51
Granite Mountain, 37
Grapefruit and Avocado Salad, 84
Grape Leaves Stuffed with Hill Country
    Lamb, 97
Grilled Catfish and Black Bean Chimichangas
    with Avocado Mayonnaise, 97
Guacamole, 76
  recipe, 78
Guadalupe Mountains National Park, 12
Gulf Coast, 21-22

Hardin, John Wesley, 56
Hays, Jack, 56
Highland Lakes, 36
Hill Country, 35-36
Hogg, Ima, 66
Hogg, James Stephen, 66
"Home on the Range" (song), 54
Hopkins, Sam (Lightnin'), 54
Houston, 23-25
Houston, Sam, 23, 26, 49, 63
Houston Ship Channel, 25

Impatiens, 119
Independence, Alamo battle and, 49
Indian blanket (wildflower), 108
Indians
    missions and, 47
    Texas name originated by, 43-46
    See also specific Indians
Institute of Texan Cultures, 40

Jackson, Andrew, 63
Jalapeños, 76
  cornbread with, 86
Jefferson, 27
Jefferson, Blind Lemon, 54
Jennings, Waylon, 54
Johnson, Lady Bird, 36, 102
Johnson, Lyndon B., 25, 40, 59
Jones, George, 54
Joplin, Scott, 54
Jordan, Barbara, 63
Jordan, Ruthmary, 99-100
Juárez, Mexico, 13
Juneteenth, 51

Kalanchoe plant, 119
Karankawa Indians, 22
Kelleher, Herb, 30
King, Richard, 17

King Ranch, 17-18
King Ranch Chicken, 86-87
Kiowa Indians, 52

Laffite, Jean, 22
Laguna Madre, 17
Lamar, Mirabeau B., 35
Language, 59-60
Leadbelly (Huddie Ledbetter), 54
Lee, Robert E., 17
Lemon Almond Muffins, 100
Lemon-mint (wildflower), 108
Lexicon, 59-60
Lipscomb, Mance, 54
Live oak trees, 116
Los Dos Laredos, 18
Lubbock, 33
Ludwig II (king of Bavaria), 63

McCulloch, Ben, 56
Mansfield Cut, 17
Marcus, Herbert, 29
Margaritas, 76
Marigolds, 119
Martinez, Matt, 72
Matamoros, Mexico, 17
Maverick, Samuel Augustus, 59
Mayonnaise, avocado, 97
Meat
    chicken-fried steak, 90
    lamb in grape leaves, 97
Mesquite, 116
Mexican hat (wildflower), 108
Mexico, independence from, 49
Michener, James, 42
Missions, Indians and, 47
Mixed Fresh Garden Greens, 99
Morgan, Emily, 49
Moss verbena (wildflower), 108
Mountain laurel tree, 116
McCulloch, Ben, 56
Mansfield Cut, 17
Marcus, Herbert, 29
Margaritas, 76
Marigolds, 119
Martinez, Matt, 72
Matamoros, Mexico, 17
Muffins
    bran spice, 100
    lemon almond, 100
Munson, T. V., 92
Music, 54-56

NASA Manned Spacecraft Center, 25
National Wildflower Research Center, 102
Neiman, Carrie, 29
Nelson, Horatio, 65
Nelson, Willie, 54
Ney, Elisabet, 63
Nimitz, Chester H., 65

Oak tree, 116
Oil, 26
Orange, 26

Padre Island, 17
Padre Island National Seashore, 18
Paintbrush (wildflower), 111
Palmito Ranch, 17
Palo Duro Canyon, 32
Panhandle Plains, 30-33
Parker, Cynthia Ann, 46
Paseo del Rio (San Antonio), 38
Peach Bread Pudding with Lemon Sauce, 99
Pecan tree, 116
Peggy's Pralines, 89
Picante, 76
Pickett, Bill, 57
Pickled Okra, 90
Piney Woods, 26
Pink evening primrose, 108
Poppy Seed Dressing, 85
Port Aransas, 21
Port Arthur, 26
Porter, William Sydney (O. Henry), 66
Pralines, 76
    recipe, 89
Price, Ray, 54
Pride House (bed-and-breakfast inn), 99-100
Primrose, 108
Pyles, Stephen, 94

Queen Isabella Causeway, 17

Ranches, 32-33
Red Pepper Sauce, 94
Red River Raft, 27
Rincon de Santa Gertrudis, 17
Rio Grande Valley, 13-17
Ritter, Tex, 54
River Walk (San Antonio), 38
Rodeos, 57-59
Roosevelt, Franklin D., 21
Roses, 119
Routh, Baby, 94

Salads
    grapefruit and avocado, 84
    mixed green, 99
    poppy seed dressing for, 85
Salsa, 76, 78
San Antonio, 37
"San Antonio Rose" (song), 54
Santa Anna, Antonio Lopez de, 23, 49
Sauces
    for chicken, 87
    lemon, 99
    red pepper, 94
    salsa, 78
Saucy Salsa, 78
Seafood
    grilled catfish, 97
    shrimp quesadillas, 94
Shrimp Quesadillas with Red Pepper
        Sauce, 94
Slavery
    freed slaves in cavalry, 52
    music, 54
Solis, Jose de, 47
South Texas Brush Country, 17-18
Southwest Airlines, 30
Spaniards
    empresario system under, 47

rodeo tradition from, 57
State Fair of Texas, 30
Statehood, 10
Staub, John, 66
Strait, George, 54

Tacos, 76
Tamales, 76
Taylor, Elizabeth, 81
Terrain, 10
Texas
    Anglo-American settlers, 49
    botanical diversity, 102
    dialect and lexicon, 59-60
    early boundaries, 10
    early European settlers in, 52
    historical claims on, 10
    origin of name, 43-46
    statehood, 10
Texas bluebonnet, 108
Texas Folklife Festival, 40
Texas Indian Campaign, 46
Texas paintbrush (wildflower), 111
Texas Rangers, 56
Tex-Mex cooking, 71-72
    glossary, 74-76
Tickseed (wildflower), 111
Togo, Heihachiro, 65
Tolbert, Frank X., 78
Tolbert's Bowl of Red, 78
Tortillas, 76
Tostadas, 76
Trans Pecos region, 12-13
Trees, 116
Tubbs, Ernest, 54
Tyler roses, 114

University of Texas, 10

Vaughan, Stevie Ray, 54
Vegetables, pickled okra, 90

Walker, Jerry Jeff, 54
Walker, Samuel H., 56
Wallace, W.A.A. "Big Foot," 56
Waller, Edwin, 36
Webb, Walter Prescott, 56
Whooping Cranes, 21
Wildflowers
    cultivation of, 107-8
    decorating with, 111
    on display, 111
    East Texas springtime shows, 114
    major species, 108-11
Willow tree, 116
Wills, Bob, 54
Wine, 92-94

"Yellow Rose of Texas" (song), 49
Ysleta Mission, 13

Xeriscape gardening, 105

Zinnias, 119